A Baby Boomer's Encounters

A Baby Boomer's ENCOUNTERS

*How Important
Contemporaries Taught Me*

J.A. PATRINA

Copyright © 2019 by J.A. Patrina.

All rights reserved. No part of this book may be reproduced in any form or by any electronic or mechanical means, including information storage and retrieval systems, without permission in writing from the publisher, except by reviewers, who may quote brief passages in a review.

This publication contains the opinions and ideas of its author. It is intended to provide helpful and informative material on the subjects addressed in the publication. The author and publisher specifically disclaim all responsibility for any liability, loss, or risk, personal or otherwise, which is incurred as a consequence, directly or indirectly, of the use and application of any of the contents of this book.

ISBN: 978-1-7330672-5-6   [Paperback Edition]

Please visit *hoodwinked.net* to discover other related writings on matters discussed within this manuscript.

Printed and bound in The United States of America.
Published by LittleHouse Enterprises Inc.

Contents

Year	Entry	Page
1980	Abbie Hoffman	13
1991	Jackie Kennedy	17
1974	Herb Reed	20
1978	Hilly Crystal	23
1971	Miles Davis	28
1965	Old Tomato Face	32
1971	The NSKK	37
1985	Woody Allen	45
1975	Art K	53
1970	Bill Graham	58
1976	Professor B	62
1978	Debra Harry	66
1978	Abe Ribacoff, et al	70
1972	The Russians	77
1978	Ella Grasso	82
1978	Bear	87
1974	James Cotton	93
1981	Madonna	105
1982	Jake LaMotta	110
1986	Big Guy	117
1980	Reggie Jackson	122
1989	Claus Peshek	128
1984	Memphis Ward Schaeffer & the Cabbies	135
1985	Muhammad Ali	143
1987	Howard Cosell	148
1988	The French	153
1987	Steve Martin (With Joey Ramone)	158
1984	Ed Koch	164
1986	Mike Tyson	167
1994	Claus Von Bulow	172
1997	Richard Gere	176
2004	Alan King	181
1997	Janette Carter	186
1996	Princess Diana	196
1999	Eric Clapton	201
1998	Ahmet Ertegun	209
1991	Bill Clinton	215
1999	Les Paul	220
2000	Ricky Martin	227
2001	Yoko Ono	233
2005	The Japanese	238
2003	Rod Stewart	247
2002	The Mob	256
2011	The Hampton's (With The Clintons)	264
2008	Walter Cronkite	269
2015	Johnny Winter	273
2014	Bill Cosby	282
2012	Jerry Adams	289
2014	Gregg Allman	295
2014	Ricky Henderson	304
2015	Odell Becham Jr	309
2016	Rudy Giuliani	316
2007	Tom Brokaw	322
2018	Van Morrison	328

THE AUTHOR

   Enclosed are personal encounters that helped shape my destiny. Most of them involve famous people, some are autobiographical occurrences, all leaving their imprint. With me as Forrest Gump, baby boomers can peak back in time to revisit their once unfettered lifestyles.

PROSPECTS—
"A BOOMER'S LIFE"

What were my prospects? I was born, 1952, a Catholic in Queens NYC, a descendent of Irish, German and Italian immigrants who until then still hovered around New York City. Being the first baby-boomer born to the family, I was a witness to my twentieth century ancestors, watching them strive to fuel the family's "upward mobility", one gritty generation at a time.

This accolade includes my own parents who, throughout the formative years, did their best to foster my American dream. And then suddenly, after doing all they could, at around 16-years old, it dawned on me: It's my turn!

My prospects? I would make the world my oyster, starting out as a musician and take it from there. After all, even if not from the "greatest generation", I was still an American, starring at open highways spanning out in front of me. And so my journey began—a blank slate about to be etched upon.

It's easy to understand—with me being a baby-boomer—why *Forrest Gump* is one of my favorite movies. I watch it every other year and cry often while under its spell. Aside from evoking America's ebbs and flows during my lifetime, the film reawakens my own Gump-like encounters which occurred without rhyme or reason across my 60-odd years.

The list of unintended encounters is quite something. How did these happen to a nobody like me? For the most part, those encountered barely cared about me any more than the important people in Forrest's life cared about him. But like Gump, these face-to-face, in-the-flesh encounters taught me something, maybe not much, but something… about my counterpart, about myself, about my times and about the journey of life.

Enclosed are my encounters.

And that's all I've got to say about that.

Not The World's Greatest Generation

Music & Lyrics by J.A. Patrina

When I was young I thought life was long.
Every day I got a brand new song.
Ran through the fields, ran through the meadow.
Filled my head with mellow yellow.

Taught to believe in our liberties.
Never mix with authority.
We loved the trees and loved the rain.
But we loved good livin' just the same.

And we're not the world's greatest generation.
No we're not the world's greatest generation.
We're a whole lotta trouble with the petal to the metal,
But we get it over the line.
A whole lotta trouble with the petal to the metal,
But we get it over the line.

Here I am with my baby doll.
She's still in love with me somehow
Open up your pretty eyes.
Stare at me up through the sky.
Up through the sky.

We ditched the commies and World War III
Still stuff keeps coming from across the sea
Four of us have come to power
And so far you know it's look'n pretty sour

And we're not the world's greatest generation …

INDEX

WOMEN
1991 — Jacqueline Kennedy
1996 — Lady Diana
1997 — Janette Carter
2001 — Yoko Ono

MEN
1970 — Bill Graham
1978 — Hilly Crystal
1979 — Bear
1987 — Howard Cosell
1994 — Claus Von Bulow
1997 — Richard Gere
2004 — Alan King
2006 — Steve Martin
2007 — Tom Brokaw
2008 — Walter Cronkite
2014 — Bill Cosby

MUSICIANS
1971 — Miles Davis
1974 — Herb Reed
1974 — James Cotton
1977 — Debra Harry
1981 — Madonna
1984 — Ward Schaeffer
1998 — Ahmet Ertegun
1999 — Les Paul
1999 — Eric Clapton
2000 — Ricky Martin
2003 — Rod Stewart
2015 — Johnny Winter
2017 — Greg Allman
2018 — Van Morrison

POLITICIANS
1980 — Abbie Hoffman
1984 — Ed Koch
1991 — Bill Clinton
2012 — Jerry Adams
2016 — Rudy Guilianni

ATHLETES
1980 — Reggie Jackson
1882 — Jake LaMotta
1987 — Muhammad Ali
1986 — Mike Tyson
2014 — Ricky Henderson
2015 — Odell Beckham Jr.

CAREER MENTORS
1965 — Old Tomato Face
1975 — Art K
1976 — Professor B
1978 — Ella Grasso
1978 — Abe Ribicoff
1979 — Sol Goldman
1986 — Big Guy
1989 — Claus Peshek

FOREIGNERS
1971 — The NSKK
1972 — The Russians
1988 — The French
2002 — The Mob
2002 — The Chinese
2005 — The Japanese
2011 — The Hamptons

1980
ABBIE HOFFMAN

The word Yippie comes from the *Youth International Party* which Abbie co-founded. His string of anti-establishmentarianism remains an exceptional resume, and in 1971 he skipped bail and in doing so, America's top hippie creep disappeared. I encountered Abbie Hoffman in 1980, right when he resurfaced from his nine-year escape from the law.

In the 1960's, Abbie was everywhere, including the march on Washington D.C., his society smashing tactics culminating in the Chicago Seven trial, along with his other famous partners including, Jerry Rubin (a future stock broker), Bobby Seale of the Black Panthers, Tom Hayden (a future congressman) and others all charged with inciting riot during the 1968 Democratic Convention.

I read his 1971 book—titled, *Steal This Book*, teaching how to live for free. All of his life he wanted to be the outrageous one, the famous one, the great disrupter, a Jew with more hutzpah than other Jews.

In 1980, when he returned from hiding somewhere in upstate NY, his radical fire still burned. The problem: he had faded in the public eye, with the fires of 1960's American radicalism only smoldering, leaving him old, unimportant and broke, bitter at his generation's abandonment of the cause (his cause).

When I encountered Abbie, 1980 was just one of many long years to come attending to my cancer-stricken wife's endless episodes in New York cancer hospitals. With little money to spare, I rewarded myself with a good meal each weekend.

In the warm weather, I regularly rode Manhattan's east side number 4 "green" express train, getting on at 86th street, getting off at Canal, headed for either China Town's Mott Street or to Little Italy's Mulberry Street. South of Canal meant Dim Sum and north a bowl of "sweet sauce" linguini at Umberto's Clam House. Umberto's is where I encountered Abbie—often.

A few years' prior, the Patriarca mob family gunned down Joey (crazy Joe) Gallo at Umberto's, as Joey celebrated his 43rd birthday together with a new wife of just three weeks and his body guard (a Greek guy). So besides the great red sauce, Umberto's Clam House held a vibe.

I liked the place. I liked the sauce.

In the months before Abbie turned himself in to the police as a fugitive, I shared the *Canal Street* territory with him. Every time—for weeks on end—he'd appear, marching up and down the street wearing street person cloths, carrying an unbalanced demeanor and lugging a big chip on his shoulder.

Sitting at my Umberto's street-side table, I would glance up and there he'd be, swerving towards my side of the street, glaring at me as he chugged by. I did not realize he was still on the lamb, thinking him just a lost hippie.

During this interlude, Janna my wife, who was enjoying an eight-week break from chemotherapy—always mindful that the "treatments" were soon to start again—allowed herself like me, to cherish a bowl of to-die-for pasta, and she would ask:

Why does he do this?

I explain that there are two types of "hippies", though in common both groups hate authority.

To break authority, Abbie's group seeks anarchy, where elite leaders like him seek to sweet talk "the little people" into accepting a diminished, "drop out" socialist hive of forced equality. Guys like me simply want to get out from under the heels of institutions (like the bank I worked at), or from people with the power to lord over me in any manner (like Abbie). We want unfettered independence in running our lives. The last thing needed? new masters, as in the Who lyric: "Meet the new boss. Same as the old boss".

The funny thing about the Who reference: At Woodstock, Abbie jumped on stage during the Who's trademark show, to protest the incarceration of another radical, and was soon physically confronted by Pete Townshend who really needed no bosses.

Finally, one Sunday, while at Umberto's, I warn Janna: *Here he comes!*

Sure enough Abbie charges over and blurts out: *Traitor!*

I stare back without expression: *F… you. You would throw everyone under the bus just to keep your power gig going.*

From that summer day in 1980, Abbie and my wife Janna survive their unfortunate fates for another few years, he dies of a suicide overdose, she of everything.

And that's all I've got to say about that.

1991
JACKIE KENNEDY

Marilyn Monroe and Jackie Kennedy are the dual female icons from my youth, but Jackie was an upper east side neighbor of mine so….

After Jack Kennedy's death, and then after Aristotle Onassis's death, Jackie settled into a New York City 5th avenue apartment, across from the Metropolitan Museum of Art, a few blocks from my humble studio abode on 81st Street.

Off-and-on Jackie was in the local news, her new life traced publically for the citizens of New York to follow. Given the esteem I held her in, the periodic updates on her life, and her proximity as a neighbor ... while walking by her building on 5th, I sometimes wondered how she was doing. I once read an article claiming her net worth only $20 million—though this may not be true—thinking, "that is definitely not enough. What about the Kennedy's; what about Onassis; what about her father "Black Jack" Bouvier for God's sake?"

One cold and rainy fall afternoon in 1991, I left my apartment in a rush only to find spitting rain coming down. Rather than turning back for an umbrella and a hat, I pushed on. Coming up to the corner of 84th and Fifth, I hugged the Marymount School fence as I whipped around the corner, colliding with a woman hidden beneath an umbrella. Preparing to apologize I recognize Jackie.

I'm sorry Jackie, I had my head down against the wind. Left my umbrella at the apartment. Are you ok?

Jackie then responded in the most gracious manner possible:

Then you are from the neighborhood?

Yes, 81st.

Her words and demeanor left me so at ease that I introduced myself. And then as we shook hands to depart, knowing her full name I said: *And it is a privilege to finally meet Jacqueline Lee Bouvier Kennedy Onassis.*

Her eyes lit as I mentioned "Lee". She smiled and we were on our way.

A few years later in 1994 Jackie died of lymphatic cancer—similar to my first wife Janna's illness. Jackie's funeral, held at Saint Ignatius Loyola on Park Avenue—three blocks from my apartment—attracted thousands. I navigated the crowd, climbed the church stairs and squeezed myself into the rear vestibule. I could not hear or see much, finally accepting I would not get close to her again.

And that's all I've got to say about that.

1973
HERB REED

When I was a boy, I followed two streams of music: Rock & Roll and Doo-Wop. Rock & Roll meant, amongst others, Elvis, Little Richard and Roy Orbison. Doo-Wop meant, amongst others, The Drifters, Frankie Lyman and the Teen Agers and Herb Reed and the Platters. Eventually Rock & Roll morphed into straight Rock, and Doo-Wop morphed into vocal bands like Frankie Vale and the Four Seasons, The Temptations and others.

My encounter with Herb Reed of *The Platters* was in early 1973. I had flunked out of Fairfield University's engineering program, moved into my parent's basement, gotten into a top notch Allman Brothers cover band, and had a day job at Dumfries Tavern in Bloomfield, Connecticut—right off Interstate 91 between Hartford and Springfield. Dumfries had a large table-cloth dinning room, hotel rooms and a dinner theater. Herb Reed, an actual legend, was performing at the dinner theater.

The story starts the day before I actually met Herb. I worked the lunch shift, assigned to wait on a table of 16 franchise owners of local McDonalds restaurants. In the early days before Ray Croc the founder of McDonalds had capital, he expanded by selling franchises. At around 300 restaurants Ray could afford to open subsequent McDonalds from within, sometimes using managers, and not just using expensive franchise owners who kept most of the profit—and the rest is McDonald's history.

My luncheon table held a collection of these franchise guys, and I can assure you they were really happy duds... err dudes, eating and drinking like crazy. I hustled like heck keeping all the balls in the air. Well done French fries... no problem. Another round. Great!

At around 2:30 pm, one guy calls me over to settle up with his credit card, and upon returning, he signs the slip and hands me a $1-dollar bill, saying: *We don't believe in tips at McDonalds!*

All the men have a big laugh at this until I say: *Then go eat at your crap places where your employees have to take your crap. I don't! Now get out before I call the manager and expose you.* And they leave...quickly.

Assigned the breakfast shift the next morning, I see Herb Reed sitting in a booth.

Hey Mr. Reed what can I get you?

A coffee, four eggs sunny side up with bacon all the way (meaning toast and potatoes).

I stood there like a dope, shocked that someone can order as many eggs as they wanted. I placed the order.

Bringing the coffee, I asked how many nights he was playing.

Thursday, Friday, Saturday.

Actually I am a guitarist, and those are the nights we (my local band) play this week, that's why I only work breakfast and lunch. Saying this I felt like a dumbbell.

But you see, he had put me at ease, and my simple youth came forth: one musician in a grove with another. I told him about how close our Allman Brothers copy band was to the real thing. He asked how long I was in the band. This triggered me into telling Herb the following:

Joe: *I was auditioned for the Dickey Betts role and couldn't play one riff from any of his songs, but I got into the band anyway.*

HR: *Then you're a touch player.*

Joe: *What's that?*

HR: *Ya got your own sound. Run with it.*

And from that moment on I have. Thank-you Herb forever!

He charged the $4-dollar meal to his room and left me a $2-dollar cash tip.

And that's all I've got to say about that!

1978
HILLY CRYSTAL

CBGBs—Hilly Crystal's punk club on the Bowery in lower Manhattan—prepared me for life.

CBGB-OMFUG—an abbreviation for the kinds of music Hilly intended to feature—stood for Country, BlueGrass, Blues and Other Music For Uplifting Gormandizers (food lovers). The club, eventually called CBGBs, opened in 1973 and became the starting point for the careers of punk rock and new wave acts including the Ramones, Talking Heads, Patti Smith, Television and Blondie.

At the time, 1978/9, while I attended a Computer Processing trade school, my band still moved in the classic rock direction, playing gigs in New England, myself writing what I now consider useless compositions—organized sound with words that rhymed. CBGBs was to change all that.

What a dump! The 1970s. This is when the NYC Bowery was still the Bowery, filled with drunks on the side walk, pimps in the street and pushers in the alleys. Before entering its door, just being in the vicinity of CBGBs meant danger, and once inside, fear of the place and fear of the band on stage compounded the environmental assault.

(Ramones at CBGB's)

With punk, entertainment meant unmeasured ferocity—an assault—putting the audience in fear for their safety, all this coming from punks on stage while one stood surrounded by unsavory punks in the audience, all the punks doing anything they wanted; a version of the wild west.

A juiced-up guy named Charlie ran the sound board every time I came to see bands or to do a gig, driving speakers sounding as vast as hell, all inside a compact space—the gigantic sound impacting the night's terror

(Hilly, on the case)

On most nights Hilly booked four bands, the first going on after 10 pm, with the final band finishing at 3 or 4 am. Everyone in the audience must have been unemployed. The bands certainly were.

Stopping at the club at noon, looking to get booked, the bar tender said to drop by in the afternoon. Sure enough Hilly is there sitting at the empty bar. We talk and he gives us a slot, a Tuesday night.

When do we go on? I ask.

Don't know. Get here early.

Back home we build a set of punk music from scratch and arrive early to find the other three bands and their equipment cluttered on the stage, and no sign of Hilly. That's when we found out… Hilly does not assign time slots; the bands fight it out. What a jungle system!

Punk aggression and punk thievery reside in all forms of rock music; just read about the Beatles in Hamburg. Many rock musicians become musicians as much for the lifestyle as for the art, but in the case of Punk, the art is even less of a priority, and the rough guy lifestyle dominates.

One time at CBGBs we ran into the Cleveland band, *Cheetah Chrome and the Dead Boys*. Cheetah wore leopard spandex and high heels. One of my guys—Jack—had something to say about it. No one got hurt.

I am happy to report that at our CBGB gigs we either went on second or third. To other bands, I pitched the fallacy that record producers like to see the final act, and one of the bands would always go for it. If another band got aggressive and wanted slot three, fine. We get slot two. Going on at midnight seemed perfect, but 1:30 am was good too. The poor band who sat and listened to these negotiations got slot one.

Hilly moved us up to Thursday and then to the weekend. For Saturday night we came out as "The Racket", two bass guitars, me wailing on lead and our drummer initially stuffed in a garbage can screaming, all of this nonsense blasting through the sound system from hell.

The audience takes the bait. A whole bunch of guys charge the stage chanting "You guys suck. You guys suck. You guys really, really suck" over and over again. The more they protest the more far out I wail on my Les Paul guitar. We kick Jack and the garbage can into the crowd and go on to play a short 30-minute set.

As the next band sets up Hilly comes up and says: *Great job boys. I want you back for the 4th* (his big Saturday, July 4th show).

And That's all I've got to say about that.

1971
MILES DAVIS

Music is the constant in my life. It starts with John Burke, my Grandfather, a post WWI boogie woogie pianist. In the 1930's he frequented *Toots Shore's* jazz club in Manhattan. John and Toots met while in the trenches of France in 1917. As a 1950's baby in our Queens, New York apartment, I stood next to John Burke as he played, sometimes annoying him by hitting the keys uninvited.

At age seven, I saw a Japanese kid pianist on the *Ed Sullivan Show*. I begged and eventually convinced my mother to hire a piano teacher. I was launched.

Then, in the 60's *Herb Albert and the Tijuana Brass* hit it big and my parents allowed me a trumpet and a trumpet teacher.

By age 15, I moved to guitar, learning to play on a nylon model my father bought home from Mexico. Next, I picked tobacco at local farms and bought myself a Fender electric. Today as a singer/songwriter, all three disciplines—keys, horns and guitar—are essential tools of my trade.

But it was not until 1971 when I encountered Miles Davis—as far out a musician/composer who has had ever lived—that I learned where music comes from... and it is not from us mere mortals.

In those years, officially, I attended Fairfield University in Connecticut. But in reality my whole life centered on running my cover band, playing gigs at regional colleges, going to the Capitol Theater in Port Chester New York to see the greatest Rock Bands of the era, and also, participating in the student committee engaged in hiring national acts to perform at Fairfield. To keep the reader from wondering, I should add that as a result of my priorities I only lasted two years at Fairfield, never going to the library even once!

We hired Miles for something like $8,000. He was to bring in his six-piece band and play a whole show in front of a few thousand people. Tickets quickly sold out.

The day of the show I bop in and out of the student center to catch the setup of incoming gear: Front of House Sound, Monitors and Lighting. Energy builds as sound and lighting units are line tested. At some point the band members arrive with a road manager of sorts. After 30 minutes of the guys joking around I ask the manager: *Where's Miles?*

Oh he's in the car. He be here soon.

The band goes on stage and does a sound check sounding like a million bucks. Again I go up to the manager and say: *The doors are now open, hope Miles is almost here.*

The place fills up and still no Miles. The band is brought out and introduced, going into a few routine numbers and I keep looking at the manager.

It's cool man. It's cool, he assures me. *Miles is getting ready.*

Ready? Where is he getting ready?

Stay cool. Don't worry.

I am off on the side of the stage watching the band and suddenly Miles blows past me with another guy, trumpet in hand, sun glasses shinning, and walks on stage to a huge reception. He starts playing the most beautiful, far out stuff I ever heard—more a stream of consciousness -but he appears in another world. Ah ha, Heroin! The band committee had discussed this but figured Miles was cool, and he was.

After a couple more numbers, Miles, nodding his head up and down hearing an inner rhythm, walks off past me and I ask: *Is that it, four numbers?*

I couldn't really see his eyes with the sun glasses, but he gave me a big smile and said: *Hey man it's cool!*

The next day we read the contract. Miles was to be paid just for showing up. We got over it quickly as the committee realized that music flowed through Miles from somewhere else, probably heaven, and on that night, four numbers was God's allotment.

And that's all I've got to say about that!

1965
OLD TOMATO FACE

In a later segment we will encounter the NBC News anchor *Tom Browkaw* who wrote *The Greatest Generation*, a book about those *peerless* Depression and World War II era Americans who overcame endless struggles. Who can argue against the premise?

In 2010 I wrote a classic rock song called <u>Not</u> *the World's Greatest Generation* about my generation, the baby boomers. Although it did not refute Brokaw's view, the song does stick up for my fellow lucky stiffs.

Lucky yes, but one noteworthy thing most baby boomers have in common is a work ethic, and this essay *Old Tomato Face* highlights our worker bee trait. Plus, *Old Tomato Face* proves the first encounter to make a dent in me beyond my parents, grand parents, aunts and uncles, and so I consider him a mentor.

It is hard to remember, but during the 1960s children still worked. There was a $1.25 minimum wage in force, but that applied to those over 16 years of age. Conversely, for those engaged in farm labor between the ages of 13 and 15, the going rate in Connecticut hovered at .85 cents an hour—$30 a week.

In my neck of the woods, northern Connecticut, a special cigar tobacco called "shade tobacco" grows like crazy, and back then, child labor from Connecticut and elsewhere worked the fields.

Cigars require three different tobaccos: 1) the main filler leaves, 2) strong binder leaves to hold the filler together, and 3) the silky, perfumed wrapper leaves, the ones you see when looking at a cigar, the ones we cultivated and harvested in "Tobacco Valley".

Our male and female work force consisted of townies like me, plus Florida kids who lived in dormitories. Fully grown Puerto Rican men also came north each year living separately. Girls worked the barns, boys the fields.

In prior years' kids from Georgia came north for work, Martin Luther King, Jr. the most famous. Martin worked farm #1. In my day I worked farm #2, though they shuttled kids back and forth between farms to keep the labor force synchronized with the development stages of the plants.

The nineteen sixties featured massive pesticides, but more, we were picking tobacco, tar and nicotine laced tobacco. As one picked the leaves, the tobacco sap splattered over you from head to toe: the nicotine turning one's skin yellow, the black tar drying on top of the nicotine. When peeling off the tar, the yellow stained skin remained.

We were 13, 14 and 15. I told you we worked.

The boss of farm #2 was Don B, but back then we only knew him as *Old Tomato Face*, our slave driver. We had straw bosses too (the Puerto Rican men patrolling the fields), but Old Tomato Face surfaced with his pickup truck whenever needed.

Shade tobacco plants grow under cheese cloth suspended ten feet off the ground by a matrix of cedar poles and crossing wires. The cloth reduces direct sunlight on the leaves keeping them supple while trapping the humidity inside—great for the plants, horrible for anyone covered with tar and nicotine.

The distance between cedar poles is called a "bin". In 1965 one got .85 cents an hour by picking up to 90 bins a day. Above 90 one received .10 cents for each additional bin. A veteran picker who hustled all day could reach 120 bins in a day—an extra $3 dollars in "piece work" pay.

Our kid leaders were two southern black boys—Lexington and Washington (not kidding). One fine morning they urged all of us to go whole hog. It turned into a race. At 11 am the straw bosses flush us out of the field, and up drives Old Tomato Face.

He throws a basket of broken leaves at us claiming that our recklessness ruined the day's yield leading to docked hours for the lot of us.

Another time, due to bad weather, the farm was almost a week behind the pace of the plants; the leaves were getting too big and tough. We picked in the pouring rain all morning, finally climbing onto the steamy bus at noon covered by mud, tar and nicotine, looking for our soggy lunches.

The bus stays quiet.

You know, we don't need to go back out, I mention to Lexi.

What you say'n?

We'll tell Jose (a straw boss) to bag it this afternoon and start again tomorrow.

Lexi tells Washington who loves the idea, and Washington tells Jose who leaves the bus. Now we become rebels. One kid draws a round tomato face on the left front window and another spells "Old Tomato Face" on the other big window. This turns into actual chanting and euphoria.

Suddenly the bus door is kicked open. Old Tomato Face climbs the steps throwing down 50 plastic ponchos.

Grab one and get off the bus. We're picking those leaves now.

We all got up and went back to work.

Welcome to the world!

Years later, while in college, I again worked for Old Tomato Face for a few weeks in June, getting the seedling beds watered. I found him to be a real person, Don B., poor, living in a tobacco company farm house, with kids of his own for whom he cared deeply. One of his boys made it into West Point.

And that's all I've got to say about that.

1971
THE NSKK

BRIDGEPORT POST July 5, 1974—Hartford, Ct. Cops Hurt in Clash with Cycle Club—*Three Hartford policemen were injured and nine arrested Tuesday following a clash between the police and the NSKK motorcycle club.*

Ah… boys will be boys. Personally, I never met the NSKK in Hartford. Instead, I encountered them in Springfield, Mass. and in Willimantic, Ct, two wonderful places one should certainly visit: p.s. bring your kids.

My NSKK experience took the form of a complex double encounter, a precious rarity actually, so here goes…

To start, this NSKK moniker comes from the 1930's Nazi unit specializing in motor cycles and trucks... ok? So it happens that some 1970's cyclists in Connecticut like bikes and trucks and adopt NSKK... ok? It's a free country! Just to warn the reader, these guys are what is called "NG"—that's "No Good". The first encounter, November, 1971:

I have three fourth row tickets to see the Allman Brothers Band in an old 1,500 seat theater in Springfield, Massachusetts, and am surprised the show still stands. Only days ago Duane Allman dies on his motor cycle in Macon Georgia.

This tragedy for all... losing Duane, a guitar virtuoso as organic, fluid and soaring as can be hoped for... was bad enough for me, but more, how—so immediately—were The Allmans going to put on a coherent show under these chaotic circumstances?

With my friend Al, I hitch from Fairfield University to my parent's house in Simsbury, Ct., to fetch my 15-year-old brother Jim, borrow a car, and head for Springfield to witness this moment.

Arriving we race down the isle to claim our 4th row center seats and encounter an immovable object: The NSKK, with 50 bikers sitting up front. I race back to the lobby to complain of intruders in my seats and am told to *talk to that guy*, a dude in a stylish leather jacket who was the show promoter, a guy named Jim Koplick (Photo: Jimmy, in the early years).

I tell my story and show my ticket, and Koplik, an irresistible force, says: *Come with me. I'll take care of it.*

We march down the center isle, he sees the NSKK, turns to me and says: *Have your two friends sit there* (pointing to the carpet in the isle by the first row) *and I'll put you on the stage*. Smart reflexes! From that moment on, Jimmy K goes on to be a show business legend, a blessing to us fans who got to see the bands.

So as my brother Jim and friend Al sit in the isle, I follow Koplick up the stairs. Jim K deposits me next to the bass rig of Allman bassist Berry Oakley (who a year later also dies by motor cycle in Macon). Next thing I know, the band is announced and they all come flowing past me. Greg Allman sits across the stage, his Hammond Organ facing me, Dickey Betts holds center stage between the drummers Jaimo and Butch Trucks.

They launch Statesboro Blues—a Duane Allman masterpiece on slide guitar—and I think I am hearing the now deceased Duane. No, its Dickey, playing Duane's riffs to a T, with Duane's touch, truly amazing. And when it's time for Dickey's solos, suddenly Dickey sounds like Dickey.

This is how the whole show goes down. Years later, I hear from legend *Rick Derringer*, that *Johnny Winter*, a distinguished signature-style guitarist as there ever was, could also play like anyone else (Johnny and Rick D above), and now I witness Dickey's sheer virtuosity, one of the most stupendous moments of my concert going years.

And to some degree those guys in the 4th row get credit for my good fortune, not to mention Koplick (thanks again Jimmy)! So the show ends and the boys file past me, Dickey last in line, big smile on his face.

Joe: *Richard, you really held the fort tonight. I could never be more impressed.*

Dickey: *Thanks. I knew all the parts, but it comes at you pretty fast. Here, keep this.*

He hands me his guitar pick, which I still have. So much for NSKK encounter #1. My next encounter with the NSKK is more intimate.

Two years later my country rock band *Fat Boy's Lunch* starts to climb, getting opening act gigs for national headliners who barrel through Connecticut. But these good gigs are few and far between, so I agree to play with my high school band mates in a blues-oriented bar band to fill the open weekends. We get a Thursday, Friday, Saturday slot at a bar in Willimantic, Connecticut, out in the middle of nowhere.

Arriving on Thursday we are ready to go by 9 pm for a 9:30 pm start. The problem, no one is there, no one! At 10 pm no one is there. At 10:30 I walk to the bar area and ask the bar tender if we should call it a night.

Bar Tender: *They'll be here.*

Joe: *Who will be here?*

Bar Tender: *You'll see.*

At eleven pm a distant rumble turns into the roar of a 747 as fifty (50) NSKK bikes arrive at "their bar". *Holy s—t, what did we get ourselves into?* Suddenly every table is full with the same guys I must have "met" at the Allman Brother's show, the difference: here they brought some of their "chicks", whereas at the Allman's must have been "boy's night out".

So we get playing with our loose, saucy blues jam sound. I am using a Bassman amp that I borrowed, and it sounds incredible, getting my lead work up to an A+ level. My childhood BFF Jack, on mic, is his irreverent, antiestablishmentarian self, and the NSKK loves the whole thing. We play two sets and it is now 1:15 am.

Joe, to the bar tender: *Ok that wraps it up for tonight* (in Connecticut, bars close by 1:30).

Bar Tender: *You can't leave now. They just got here.*

Joe: *Oh, how long do we play.*

Bar Tender: *Until they leave.*

Joe: *Ok, I get it.*

On Friday and Saturday, we agree to arrive just before 11 pm and play till 3 am, just to put some structure around it, and the bar tender gets the ok from the gang leader for this. Saturday night around 2 am, I'm at the bar and the gang leader comes up saying they want us back next weekend. Seeing that no one has been murdered, Jack, my bandmate, and I say yes.

The following weekend turns into a third weekend. The NSKK boys love us, hopefully not to death. They especially love our version of *300 Pound Fat Momma*, and the top gang guys finally approach us.

Gang guy 1: *We want you to be our permanent band.*

Gang guy 2: *Yea you can hang out at our compound.*

Gang guy 3: *And can have our chicks too.*

I explain that I am in *Fat Boy's Lunch,* with shows the next few weeks, but that it is a good offer, and we would call.

We never call. Admittedly, us and the NSKK share some actual overlap in living free, in despising authority, and in being unencumbered old-school "Daniel Boone" Americans. But those commonalities represent just a segment. Overall, we are not symmetric, and so, we never call.

And that's all I've got to say about that.

P.S. Twenty-five years later I am in a limo with two other couples, including my sister Carol and husband Ken, going to a 'happening' eastern Connecticut farm that serves farm-to-table cuisine. Riding in the car is Tony S, a friend of ours, who then worked for my company Wall Street Systems in New York. Tony S had gone to Yale, and became our contract administrator.

As we drift through the empty woodland roads of rural Connecticut, soon I remember the NSKK, wondering if they are still intact, and I tell my story to everyone. Tony S, who owns a Harley, jumps in:

Tony: I was in the NSKK back then. I know the bar.

All: *What?*

Tony: *Yea. I fixed everyone's bikes in the gang, going to Yale at the same time. The guys called me "Doc". It was best you never called them. Once in, it's hard to get out!*

1985
WOODY ALLEN

Readers of my encounters may notice that most of them happened in New York City. This outcome did not come about simply by moving there; it happened because I chose New York as my beacon of opportunity, and once there, I stood ready to engage with and learn from other New Yorkers. Location, location, location!

As you will see, I landed on the upper east side of Manhattan back in 1979, and upon finding my "good luck" rent-controlled apartment on the corner of 81st Street and Park Avenue, I could only assume that divine intervention had purposely placed me there. And so, over the next thirty years, in order not to break my "location, location, location" destiny, I rented three apartments, all on East 81st Street, refusing to move off the block.

I know this sounds peculiar for those never entangled within the spider web of the Big Apple, but East 81st and East

80th will remain my favorite pavements until I die. And I mean pavements. I revere those streets.

I am a New York idiot. I love the place. As the elevator door opens, I can run into a neighbor from the sixth floor who I somehow appreciate. I next greet the doorman in the lobby. Outside, I know all the shop owners in the vicinity, and most of all I know every proprietor of every deli, coffee shop, pizza parlor and fine restaurant within the endless blocks of my stinking small apartment. You see, New York is really a warm place, filled with human contact. Conversely, these days, in the suburbs, I move around from parking lot to parking lot, never interacting with anyone.

Ok, where does Woody Allen, born in Rockaway, Queens, NYC, near the airport, fit in with all of this? Everywhere! He is the ultimate New Yorker.

Correction … not quite everywhere. Woody lives further south of me on 5th and 74th. But there is a common denominator bringing us closer, Woody's best friend, the Broadway actor Tony Roberts, who lives in my neighborhood. Woody always hangs with Tony.

Now in Woody's film *Annie Hall*, it is Tony Roberts who marches up and down New York's avenues as Woody spills his guts out about Diane Keaton, Woody's girlfriend (photo: all three). In these scenes, Tony patiently listens to Woody's neurotic dribble.

Most think the Annie Hall dialogues came from the movie's screen play, with Woody and Tony doing real, important acting. Nope: *this was them throughout the 1980's, strolling NYC like the rest of us, with Woody perpetually a wreck, frantic, looking up at the taller Tony as they patrolled the streets.*

For Annie Hall, they simply filmed one of these many moments of reality.

Being poor in the 1980's—meaning I had no money—meant that every Saturday and Sunday I too covered a lot of ground, especially on the so called Upper East Side, and so, over the years, I must have seen these two roaming kooks thirty or forty times. I guess this makes me a freak'n expert on Woody Allen and Tony Roberts. What a lasting legacy for me.

But I do not categorize these haphazard sightings as true encounters. In the end, there was only one fleeting moment pertaining to Woody that for multiple reasons I will keep for life, as you will soon see.

First, let's appreciate Woody.

Woody, one of many important New York Jewish comedians, blossomed around 1960, right after the standup greats of the 1950's, guys like Alan King, Jackie Mason and Lenny Bruce. Though Woody started with stand up, his forte became film, and with film he sure mixed things up with his great "spoof" offerings that kept us in stitches for decades.

Interestingly, after Woody, along this progression of New York Jewish humorists, came Jerry Seinfeld with Jerry mastering television.

For years, us boomers attended "Woody Allen nights" showing three or four of his films in a row, like: *Bananas, Every Thing You Ever Wanted to Know About Sex, Sleeper* and *Love and Death*.

After a while though, Woody began making films like *Manhattan* and *Hannah and Her Sisters*. With these, Woody moved away from commercial entertainment into self-medicated psychotherapy films. This is when I dropped out. But it was a hell of a run until then.

One more thing. Woody was always a serious musician. He played clarinet Monday's at a jazz club in The Village, though,

to my regret, I never went down there to catch his act and therefor certainly lost the chance of getting to know him. Instead, my only direct encounter with Woody follows.

After a grey winter, New Yorkers, like everyone else, can't wait for the first signs of spring. Finally, one can really get out there and hit the pavement which temporarily basks in a combination of cool air and hot sun. Other times of the year the concrete can be dreadful. Photo, typical couple.

So it is mid-April, just past Easter, with Janna, my first wife, enjoying one of her last viable years of life. Her cancer is in "remission", she is not currently polluted with chemo, and we are out and about, claiming our turf like all the rest of them.

For breakfast, we first head for the Plaza Hotel on Central Park South, and afterwards stroll north on Madison, returning towards our East 81st neighborhood.

By this time of the day, Madison Avenue is wall to wall, like it always is on these glorious spring weekends. Both sides of the avenue are a crush of people moving in north and south directions.

On the side we traverse, those walking south hug the retail shop windows, those waking north (ourselves) flow against the cars parked at parking meters along the road.

Even with this two-way pattern in place, one is not on easy street, as the people in the south lane perpetually collide with the people in the north lane, sending shock waves throughout the respective lanes. Janna and I walk, my arm around her, her positioned out towards the curb, me inside where the shock waves occur.

In this manner, we make our way north, block by block.

Suddenly things grind to a halt. Another couple walking south—who should be over by the shop windows—stands in our lane facing us. It's Woody and his wife Mia Farrow. Woody stands along the curb facing Janna, and Mia stands right in front of me (Mia, photo).

I must say, for the record, that both Janna and Mia are outstanding "hippie girl" beauties, and in contrast, that Woody and I appear questionable dudes—certainly lucky dudes.

But the main response of the moment remains: what the F is Woody thinking? Ten thousand of us have embraced the spring-time, side-walk parade protocol and now this. Woody, the perpetual misfit!

The four of us stop and stare at each other as the swirling horde struggles to by-pass us trouble makers, some pedestrians saying derogatory things. Can't they see that it's Woody? Jeeze folks, cut us some slack, you vicious, pushy Manhattan a-holes! God, I hate New Yorkers.

Finally, "wrong-direction" Woody steps off the sidewalk and into the street, pulling Mia with him, making room for Janna and I to get by, and this is when I said:

Thanks Woody.

And that's all I've got to say about that.

Below: Woody in "Sleeper". BTW, he is not acting—this is him!

1975
ART K

Way before NYC, Art K, I'll call him, affected my destiny. Here is why.

In 1974 I attended community college, worked its bookstore, ran a dynamite Allman Brothers tribute band, and drove part time for Art.

Art's business consisted of buying used cars off out-of-state dealer lots, "fixing them up" and then reselling them back to Connecticut dealers at the weekly Connecticut dealer's "wink, wink" auction, meaning: none of the dealers buying Art's cars had the heart to dissuade Art from odometer fixing (setting the mileage back).

At the time, most of my band worked for Art. Our two fold-duties: 1) drive with Art in his Limo to various car dealerships outside of Connecticut where Art would buy six cars, and 2), us guys would drive the clunkers home—bumper to bumper at 100 miles per hour on the Mass Pike without ever getting pulled over, go figure. Only one car ever blew up.

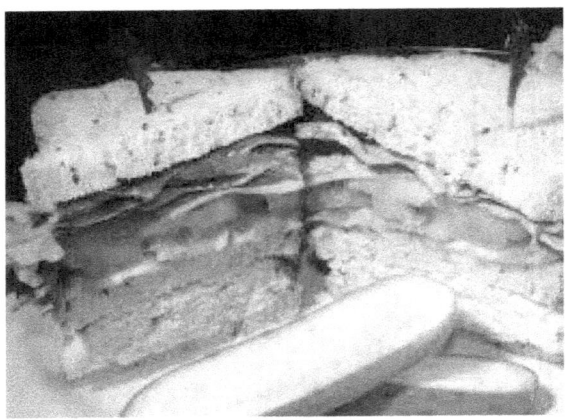

For this we each got $15 bucks and—on the way out—a big New York style sandwich at Rein's Deli off interstate 84. This constituted our daily meal. The job was perfect as we began at 11 am, and at 100 miles per hour we would be back at the band house before 3, in time for rehearsal or a local gig.

Tuesday was auction day. We drove any cars ready to leave Art's body shop over to Southern Auto Auction and jockeyed them through the auction block. Art would be at the podium with a black jack in his right hand, a microphone in his left, pounding and shouting at the cigar champing dealers across the block, smugly sitting there with their mistresses (Tuesday was also mistress day). Most wore fur coats in the cooler weather.

Driving my car onto the block I could only see Art's hand action outside the driver's window, a pounding black jack two feet from me with Art shouting: *This is a G—D--- 1973 Buick Skylark creampuff. Get off your lazy F----- asses and bid!*

Nice touch Art.

On car hunting days, one of us would drive the limo on the way out with Art sitting shotgun, chain smoking and chatting it up with "his boys" — Art being way saltier than the musician vagabonds he employed. Since Tuesday was auction day, Thursday was a day off because that was Art's day with his "pay to play girl" who "lets me do anything". But still, Art loved his boys, and always gave us advice.

He wanted me to get into Trinity College, a huge jump from the community college I slugged it out in, filled with younger Latinos and older black Viet Nam vets, and suggested I take two courses over at Trinity to prove my metal, which I did, getting two A's.

Next he said that after I got in, and because Trinity is small, I should be able to run it, just like the chickens in his old chicken farm.

You see, we had chicks hatching every day, and sometimes the older chicks would gang up on the baby chicks so we had to put the baby's in a new pen.

Then in the new pen, one of the chicks learned to become king of that pen, and we could put that chic in any other pen and it would become the king.

Thanks Art.

By the way, besides Art, I knew two other Hartford area Jewish guys that grew up on chicken farms, one guy a famous radio personality and the other a prominent lawyer. Myself, coming from the New York metropolitan area, found this hysterical.

One day in the rain, I walk from the Community College where I had just finished my final two courses, across town to Trinity, where I had simultaneously taken those initial two courses. I go to the Registrar's office and select five courses for the next semester. (Trinity photo)

The secretary looks at my form and soon comes out with the Registrar who says I cannot take five courses as I had not matriculated.

What's that?

It means that you have not been accepted by and enrolled into the school. You can take a course or two, but that can only lead to a degree if you are accepted into the school.

Well accept me.

You have to go through admissions for that.

But I just took two of your courses and got two A's and I also got two more A's at the community college. There's no question I can do the work.

He picks up the phone and says: *Tom, there's someone here I want you to meet*, and hangs up.

I want you to go downstairs to Admissions, Mr. D is waiting there for you.

Mr. D and I have a long talk, mainly about music, and I ask if he can matriculate me.

Well not right here. At the least, you will have to write the essay I described, but go home, write it and get back to me.

I guess you guys like helping students from the community.

Yes, we do.

Well besides me, I have a Puerto Rican friend you should meet. It's a guarantee he'll do fine here.

Ok.

Plus, you can consider me to be black.

What?

It's just an assumption, but part of me is Italian, and when Hannibal attacked Italy, the Elephant handlers were black guys, and some hanky-panky probably took place with the Italian girls.

He stares at me.

Look, even if I'm just a little black, at least you can get two sure-thing transfers from the community college, and the other guy is definitely Puerto Rican.

Go home and write your essay!

I got in to Trinity, and Art was pleased for me.

Soon thereafter, at 11:00 am one driving day, I and some band guys arrive at Art's body shop to go out on another mission. The body shop guys are standing there looking grim.

What's going on?

F.B.I. man, they just took Art.

On what?

90 counts of odometer fixing.

One of the band guys worried about his deli sandwich says: *You mean we're not going out?*

And that's all I've got to say about that.

1970
BILL GRAHAM

When Jack Kennedy said: *Ask not what your country can do for you. Ask what you can do for your country*, perhaps no one answered the call better then Bill Graham, a holocaust refuge, a U.S. military veteran and the greatest mentor of rock music of all time.

I had my encounter with Bill in 1970, at Tanglewood, in Lenox Massachusetts, where he was promoting Lee Michaels, Jethro Tull and The Who in concert.

I feel bad about what happened, though not at the time. Sometimes it takes distance for things to set.

I had just bought a Rambler (a car) for $200 that was an actual cream puff (ran great, no troubles ever), and our four-piece band *The Bunns*, drove up from Connecticut to Western Massachusetts without tickets or money to see the bands.

Tull, who I had seen a few times already, had just released a great work of art, the *Benefit* album, and The Who were still performing *Tommy*. Lee Michaels had his hit: *Do you know what I mean*. Besides Bill Graham's Fillmore theaters in

New York and San Francisco, Bill organized many outdoor extravaganzas, and this Tanglewood event was one.

Me and the lads are pumped, convinced we can break in somewhere across the vast perimeter fences of Tanglewood. Arriving, tons of cars and Woodstock-like traffic cause us to leave the car on a road somewhere in Lenox.

Running up, we find a huge swath of people with tickets flowing through the main entrance. We move down the twelve-foot high fence to join perhaps 100 other punks seeking, so to speak, to storm the Bastille. The problem: State troopers, around 50 of them stand guard inside. But 100 against 50 seems good. And remember, everyone of us is a complete idiot.

Something triggers the assault and 100 guys bounce onto the fence, jumping off on the other side, me one of them. Once grounded one runs like the dickens hoping the troopers can't keep up. That's when it happened.

A huge trooper suddenly lifts me by my T-Shirt and bobbles me in the air. Next a man's face sits an inch from mine. It's Bill Graham almost poking my eye: *You're ruining it for everyone!*

The Trooper drags me off. Bill gestures at me in disgust.

Thrown out into the dirt, I find my bandmates—no one got through—and one of them—Jack, of course—gets an idea. Rather then the fences, lets go through the main gate and make it look like we just showed a ticket to one of the ticket marshals, and then keep to the center and slip through.

It works, and by the time The Who come on, the four of us squirm our way down to the first row and experience what Townshend later deemed the definitive performance of "Young Man's Blues".

After the show, finding my car, all four tires are slashed. And we have no money. Bad Karma!

And that's all I've got to say about that!

Ian Anderson in action. Hailing from The Isle of Skye, in Scotland, if you can dig it.

A pure artist!

Carlos Santana & Keith Richards with Bill Graham, real achievers!

1976
PROFESSOR B

Professor B was the head of Trinity College's economics department. Upon declaring one's major inside of the economics discipline, Dr. B's "Comparative Economic Systems" class, conducted in the fall semester of one's junior year, was mandatory for all comers. This way before degree candidates drifted far astray, Dr. B could draw a bead on them, and more, leave his mark (particularly on me).

Calling him one of my mentors, though, is a stretch. He was really a disparager, but as Conan the Barbarian put it "That which does not kill you makes you stronger."

We were but seven in a small room with a blackboard. On the first day Dr. B walks in, jacket and bow tie, with a *Wall Street Journal* under his arm, which he slams down on the front desk.

You will have one of these in your possession for the remaining days of your life. See my secretary to arrange for a subscription.

Dr. B was the exact model of the "Paper Chase" professor at Harvard Law, and I sensed my 3.7 GPA in big trouble.

Next he calls role from a piece of paper.

Mr. Smith

Here

Mr. Abernathy

Here

Mr. Sykes

Here

Mr. Thomson

Here

Mr. Griffith

Here

Mr. Bates

Here

And our Italian, Mr. Patrina

Here

Well at least I was inside Trinity, rather than at the community college I had just transferred out of. Still, diversity mania had not yet taken hold within this bastion of White Anglo Saxon Protestants (W.A.S.P.s), with most of my classmates coming out of private boarding schools. At the community college I was the only white guy, and now I was the only non-W.A.S.P., still a minority, but moving up.

For the next six weeks when called upon I was the Italian, my name never spoken by the good professor. He really stressed the "I".

But the course was great. We dug into the differences between Soviet versus Chinese Communism, Western European Socialism, South American Dictatorships, American Free Market and Oligopoly Dynamics, etc. The most interesting model was the Yugoslavian system—this was before Yugoslavia disintegrated during the Bill Clinton years.

Back in the 70's Yugoslavia was still ruled by Tito, following a "true" Marxist configuration. If, say. You worked at a factory with 180 employees, each employee shared in the surplus income of the firm, whereas in Russia and China, the surplus went to the state.

Six weeks in and I am still the Italian, but then my break comes. Dr. B puts an obscure formula on the board and presents it. I had been exposed to this formula at Hartford Community College, and knew he had it wrong. I raise my hand.

Yes, the Italian.

Professor B, I think you have it wrong, isn't it…?

No, it is not ….

Class is over. Coming back two days later, Dr. B puts his Wall Street Journal down on the desk and announces.

I need to apologize to Mr. Patrina. He is correct regarding the formula.

Ok, I had my breakthrough, I finally had a name, but how was I going to ace the class. Back then I had GPA on the brain at all times, actually believing it would affect my future, so I was frantic for an idea.

One day I spoke to my father on the phone and told him about the Yugoslav system I had only just discovered. Of course he knew all about it and added that a group of Yugoslav engineers had just visited him at his company Combustion Engineering, and that they were in the area, their host: United Technologies. What a tip!

He gives me a name, and I track down the United Technology manager caring for the Yugoslav contingent.

I describe our course program, saying Trinity would be thrilled for the group to visit the economics department. A day later the answer comes back "They would love to visit Trinity".

So I line the whole thing up with all of the department professors and Dr. B, who decrees that economic majors must attend. We have the seminar, which went great, other than the minor amount of English the Yugoslavs possessed and some of the ridiculous questions posed by some of the flakey professors on our side of the discussion.

No matter, I got my "A". My GPA was safe.

Trinity's "Protestant" church

Of course this minority situation was not the last of it. I was soon to get into banking.

And that's all I've got to say about that.

1978
DEBRA HARRY

Thankfully, Punk Rock peaked around 1977, and transitioned from assault music into a softer, pop-oriented format called New Wave. With her beautiful songs, soft voice and hip look, Debra Harry (DH) and her band Blondie pioneered and exhibited the epitome of this more elegant style. As you will see, for some ridiculous reason, I thought DH—someone still relatively unknown in 1978 yet about to become a huge star—actually needed my help, and I offered it during her moment of chaos.

In the 70's a 2,000 capacity performance venue in Hartford hosted shows that included regional bands like mine as well as rising or sinking National acts like Lou Reed, Ten Years After and Blondie. My country rock band *Fat Boys Lunch* did well there in the 1974-time period. At the time a fella named Tex was our sound man. Tex owned the system and he received a full share of band revenues—a full band member who lived in the band house. Oh, yes he was from Texas.

When not gigging, Tex would rent his stuff out to other bands or to local concert venues hosting the touring acts. In 1978, when Blondie rolled in Tex got the call and rented his system out. He had just bought eight top-flight Shure microphones, and the whole rig was sweet.

The venue did all of the production work, setting up the gear, EQing the room and mixing Blondie's live show.

I show up pumped to see if Debra Harry can deliver the live goods as well as she did the studio goods. At that point DH only has her first album out, but it includes *Heart of Glass*, and *High Tide*, two masterpieces not yet hitting the radio waves, but bound to top the charts.

DH comes out, starts the show, and the audience jumps all in for what transpires, but there is consternation on stage, as Harry keeps turning to the drummer during and between songs, ignoring the audience. She becomes visibly pissed, and finally slams her microphone to the floor, breaking it. She grabs the next microphone down the line, sings for a minute and smashes that one too. Then another and another, and walks off.

Minutes pass until someone comes on stage saying the band will return once some technical difficulties are worked out. Time passes and out they come. They rave the show up a second time but DH stays visibly upset and begins smashing the microphones again.

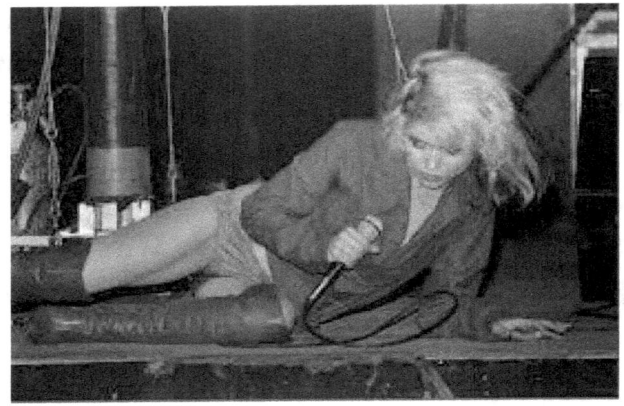

Soon all are broken, but she continues to sing through the last smashed mic, sounding like a fog horn. Horrible! She does three more songs under these conditions, probably to fulfill the contract for payment, and walks off again.

Knowing the venue, I race to the dressing room, enter and there they all are with a lot of shouting going on—a classic band fight. Unbelievably I confront DH telling her who I am, saying she should add me to her band, not just as a guitarist, but as a road manager, claiming that I would keep her from shooting herself in the foot—ever again—like I had just witnessed. She stares at me as I speak, I see through her thick makeup at her pock-marked skin and finally she says:

Who is this guy. Get him out of here!

And they did.

Thirty years later, a fella named Bobby Kuhl joins my band *LittleHouse* as sound engineer. One night we trade war stories and it ends up that Bobby was the one who rented Tex's gear and ran sound that night for Blondie. He apparently confronted DH for damaging the equipment all for nothing, as whatever conflict taking place inside the band that night had nothing to do with the sound system, but she ignored him, as did the show's promoter, as did the venue manager, and Tex lost his new gear without compensation.

Welcome to show biz!

And that's all I've got to say about that.

My favorite DH lyrics …

"Once I had a love, and it was a gas, but please don't break this heart of glass."

And…

"When I met you in the restaurant

You could tell I was no debutante

You asked me what's my pleasure

A movie or a measure?

I'll have a cup of tea and tell you of my dreaming

Dreaming is free."

1978
ABE RIBACOFF, ET AL

One short 1978 episode, amidst the Jimmy Carter recession, found me employed as a temporary Christmas clerk in the men's shop at GFOX, a department store in Hartford. I had just graduated Trinity College with excellent grades in economics with my only job offer coming from Aetna, the insurance giant. Aetna wanted me to time clerical people with a stop watch, to find more efficient methods. Having turned this horrible idea down I took the job at GFOX.

In those days, Hartford, which in the late 1800's stood as the wealthiest city in America—with residents like Mark Twain and Elizabeth Beecher Stow—held onto its past with GFOX, the pillar of downtown Hartford, its last bastion of civility. GFOX folded in 1992, but in 1978, before the malls, everyone in that part of Connecticut made their way downtown for Christmas shopping, including most of the Connecticut corporate and political dignitaries.

The men's department held prominence due to its location on the main floor right when entering the store's grand entrance. I looked forward to each day, as a stream of shoppers, including many people of stature, stopped by, sparking my interest, usually leaving the men's department with a purchase. Besides keeping shelves stocked, and everything ship shape, my main job was to greet customers, create a stylish environment to get them in the mood, help them succeed with their interests, and introduce them to other cool stuff they might not have thought of.

If no one was immediately shopping in my department, I stood at the main isle, greeting everyone entering the store: *Don't forget the men's shop.*

Over the course of my seven-week stint at GFOX's, with the above as my modus operandi, many business owners and corporate executives handed me business cards asking me to apply at their firms. *Where were they a few weeks ago!* But I really did not want to be sucked into a sales career, and never called any of them.

When one of the big guys came in it seemed the whole store knew. Harold Geneen stepped in one evening, the CEO and architect of the Hartford Fire/IT&T conglomerate consisting of around 240 discrete businesses, Harry stood small in stature, a fierce power house of a man.

Harry picked a tie, looked me in the eye and said "I'll take this". He could have meant he was buying the entire May Company who owned GFOX, but it was just the tie.

A year later, while at a data processing trade school sponsored by the insurance companies, I got a peek at Geneen's board room atop Hartford Fire's Headquarters. A vast table—looking like a football field—held a small lamp and a microphone for each reporting business president, scary!

Geneen's experiment in vast conglomeration eventually imploded.

Silver haired Abe Ribicoff came in with a small entourage looking like a member of the royal family.

(Daley)

An important guy, a former governor, now Senator, a pal of Jack Kennedy, Abe was the one who called out Mayor Daley at the 1968 convention for the gestapo tactics Daley employed in dealing with the rioting outside. On National TV, Daley could be seen saying: "F--- you, you Jew son of a bitch".

(Ribicoff attacking Daley)

I had one earlier encounter with Abe. My family, just moved from Long Island to Connecticut in 1964, was driving in our station wagon south, below Hartford, on Interstate 91. Out my window a limousine begins to pass and one of my parents says: *Look kids, it's Senator Ribicoff.* We all go to the window and wave. He sees us and raises his shaded window to put an end to the encounter.

I remembered this when he walked into the store that day, 14 years later, I perched on the main isle at GFOX.

Hello Senator thanks for coming in. Care to browse the men's department?

Thanks no. I'm shopping for others today.

That's fine, but our buyers have gone all out bringing in great merchandise this year. Those dress shirts over there are Egyptian cotton and all the guys are buying them.

Really?

He buys two, thanks me, and leaves one of his assistants to settle the bill. (Ribicoff with Kennedy)

Chris Dodd walks in one afternoon. He is up and coming in American politics. Like Al Gore, Chris is a senator's son — the kind mentioned by John Fogerty of Credence Clear Water Revival as in "I'm no senator's son". His father, Thomas Dodd was a prosecutor at the Nazi trials, and later a Connecticut Senator who was censured by the U.S. Senate for corruption.

Chris, the Senator's son, became Ted Kennedy's best friend and rumor has it that they invented something called a waitress sandwich, whatever that could mean.

Before being pushed out of politics for getting illegal loans while head of the Senate Banking Committee, Chris and Barney Frank (photo) passed the Dodd/Frank, laws intended to protect America from financial disasters. For example, unless one can prove assets of over $2 million dollars, one cannot invest in start ups.

One can go to the casino or buy state lottery tickets, but one can not invest in start ups. Brilliant.

Chris, young and tall, had a striking look. He bought a tie.

Last to mention, my old boss Art K walks in with his wife. I recognize him immediately, even with his snow white hair. Two year's prior the F.B.I. had arrested Art when he had black hair, for 90 counts of odometer fixing.

Art, it's me Joe. How are you.

Joe is that you? You look great in the blue suit. I just got out (of prison).

I look at his distraught wife who adds: *Thank God he made it!*

What are you going to do now?

Not what I was doing then.

By the way, the blue suit he referred to was purchased by me at GFOX. They had an employee discount, but the manager threw in the rest as a bonus.

And that's all I've got to say about that.

1972
THE RUSSIANS

My first experience with the communist strongmen out of Moscow came a long time ago. It was just after my 20th birthday, back in the early 1970s. At that time, I had left college to play in a rock band full time. As you can imagine, I looked the part. Now get ready, 'cause you can't make this stuff up.

I receive a call from my father, a former U.S. Navy officer who now ran a global corporate enterprise that built electric power plants all around the world. He tells me that some big Russians are on their way over to the U.S. to meet with his company about "technology acquisition", AKA licensing for you MBA types. The event might require, as he said: "your special skills..." by which he meant—I could only assume — my ability to cause trouble.

(above: Joe Sr. and Jr.)

"Who gave you permission to do this?" I want to know.

"The State Department" (then under Henry Kissinger). "They said we could talk to the Soviets, but that no deals were to be made without State Department approval."

"Wow. Where do I fit in?"

"Just get to the house Saturday afternoon. The Russian Minister of Heavy Industry and the Russian Minister of Electric Power will participate with an entourage of around 10. Your mother is having it catered. Just talk to them."

"Fine, I'll be there."

The day of their visit, a bunch of huge Russian limos pull up in front of my parents' house, and all these guys in suits step out, plus one drop- dead beautiful woman who soon I would learn would serve as interpreter. (BTW, my mother says the interpreter wasn't as smashing as I, the 20-year-old remembers her to be).

Besides the interpreter, the group included technocrats, communist party people, and, of course, KGB.

It didn't take long. I stand in the living room where the Minister of Heavy Industry, in his late 40s, tall and thin, approaches me. The fem fatal interpreter strides at once to my left side, and then my father appears to my right. I hold out my hand and greet the minister, who takes my hand. He holds it and says, through the fetching interpreter, "When I was your age, I had 500 men under me."

What, I think, no hello?

I respond by looking at the beautiful interpreter saying, "Please tell the minister that I have never had even one man 'under' me." At that point he drops my hand.

"Also please tell the minister that, yes, I am in a rock band, but that this is substantial. My band members and I are essentially business partners in an entrepreneurial venture. We invent and manufacture our own product—the music—

we go out and secure paid engagements, and then we deliver the product by performing it ourselves.

"No one helps us. We stand on our own feet, whereas you, sir, I am quite sure, have never done anything on your own. You live under the skirts of the party."

He walks off in great anger. The interpreter backs away. Certain that I screwed up royally, I turn and ask my father "Was that ok?" He says, "He attacked you".

Ok, so far so good, but still I wonder how on earth my conversation can help close the electric power deal these guys seek.

I wander into the den. The Minister of Electric Power—a spitting image of Khrushchev—spots me. He appears anxious to dismantle my very "hippy creep" existence. As he walks over, followed by the interpreter and my father, I hold out my hand to greet him. And he ...grabs my hand with his right, and with his left, reaches out and squeezes my upper arm, saying, "So, this is the strength of the American youth."

I pause, looked at my Father with a Jack Benny look, and then glance at the amazing 30-year-old beautiful interpreter.

Finally, I take my spare hand and poke this Khrushchev guy in his huge, bulging stomach, and say: "So this is the guts of the Russian leadership." (above Castro & Khrushchev)

Sometime later, upon my father's return from multiple tours of a dozen Russian power plants west of the Urals—where they fed him borsht and bread—the State Department and the CIA pulled the plug on the whole thing. And other than the fact that my father regularly met with a guy from the CIA, that's all I know. I swear.

Except that my mother, who strategized almost every move any of us ever made, including those of my father, said that there was more to it.

For instance, after the cocktail party phase of the Russian event, my mother conducts the dinner party phase, which I am not part of (read not invited to by my mother).

After the dinner, there takes place, as reported to me by many, not just my mother, the vodka phase of the event, which leads to the singing phase by the Russians.

The most important Russian engineer for electric power technology inside of the whole Soviet Union is in attendance, and, the poor soul, he decides to sing—a WWII song.

Although I was not physically at the dinner party taking place out in the breezeway room, I still hang out inside of the main house, and at one point I notice that all of the Russians are rushing up to their cars.

My mother comes in and tells me that our Ukrainian neighbor who was one of the dinner party guests (read an agent of my mother), said that the engineer's song had some disrespectful passages about the capitalistic west (this, of course, meant us—the U.S. version of us), and that as restitution, the senior minister (the Khrushchev fellow who was sent here to get a deal), pulled the plug on my mother's dinner party, and told the entourage to go to the cars.

The senior minister calls my father on Monday to say that the senior engineer had been disrespectful and that he is already back in Russia where he will be demoted for his behavior.

P.S. Thirty years later, in 2010 my family travelled to Russia, still expecting it to be as portrayed above. And you know what? It hasn't really changed.

And that's all I've got to say about that.

1978
ELLA GRASSO

One overlooked milestone in American history? Ella Grasso, the first elected female state governor in the United States. She served Connecticut from 1975 until 1980, developed cancer while in office and then died a year later. My enccunter with her took place in the spring of 1978, when I worked as a communication liaison between her office and the towns to organize cable TV districts.

It was right in the middle of the "Jimmy Carter" recession, when economically, the country had double digit everything, something Ronald Regan would explain later in 1980.

I had just graduated from Hartford's Trinity College, majoring in International Economics, and after my Christmas job at GFOX, the only full time job I could find, a state job, turned out to be an eye opener in more ways than one.

I reported to John Standish, a commissioner of public utilities, who often reminded me that he was a direct descendent of Miles Standish. John wanted to be governor some day and told me: *My family has been running Connecticut since the Indians.*

Maybe, should I decide to enter politics, I could be useful in helping him.

At first I did not realize I had already entered politics. My job was to set up meetings with the towns, drive each day to a meeting and explain the economies of scale and other practical matters of setting up cable companies and networks. The state planned to award contracts to various companies within the cable districts someone had drawn up on the state map.

In my naivety, I did not see two glaring political footballs: which towns are in which district, and what cable company gets each district.

These kinds of commercial/power topics, I soon realized, are exactly what politics is all about once one gets elected. Citizens only hear about pretend issues, and even then, only during election season.

Each day I went to the state car garage across from the capitol, got my car, drove to one of the towns, found the conference room, and there they all were… every figurehead from the town *du jour:* the fire guy with his uniform, the police guy with his, the building guys in low key jackets and ties, the board of education guy in a bow tie, the mayor always looking sharp, and others from the town republican and democrat committees.

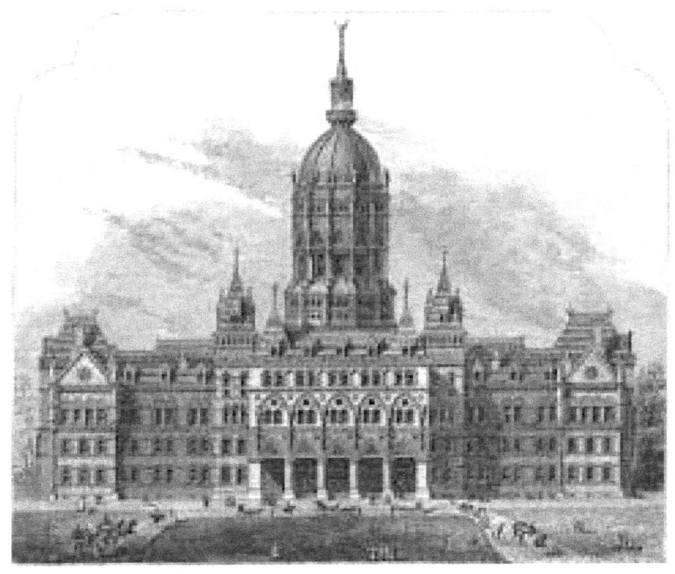

I could not imagine they wanted to meet with me! (above: Ct. Capitol)

It finally dawned on my pea brain that in their eyes I represented the state capitol, the governor, a level of government they could only dream of. Therefor I, Joe Patrina, must be one of the governors up-- and--coming players. I did not explain that I did this due to not finding a real job.

My best moment came out of a visit to Greenwich, the richest town in America.

I would say 25 Greenwich people showed up, led by a fiery mayor, a big guy, an Italian guy, someone who liked my style (this was my 47th town meeting). I was poised and fluent, already comfortable walking into the unknown and dealing with what came next. I wore my blue suit from GFOX, white shirt and tie, looked like a million bucks, and if I wanted to I could--a--been a player. Who knows, maybe Standish's right hand guy!

There was a lot of give and take about Greenwich not wanting to be in the same district as Stamford. Finally, the mayor stands up and orders me to listen closely and to personally tell Grasso the following…

The next day Standish brings me to the governor's office, saying I had just been to Greenwich and needed to report something.

Grasso: *So you met Mayor X?*

Joe: *Yes, and about 25 others.*

Grasso: *And?*

Joe: *He wants me to convey something very specific that he said in the meeting.*

Grasso: *In front of the others?*

Joe: *Yes*

Grasso: *Ok, let's have it.*

Joe: *He said, "The town of Greenwich wants nothing to do with those pornography loving people over in Stamford. Greenwich wants its own cable company and doesn't give a f… about economies of scale. Greenwich will cover the whole bill."*

Grasso: *Fine. I'll give him a call.*

(above: a house in Greenwich)

And that's all I have to say about that.

1978
BEAR

After graduating from Trinity College, my foray into punk rock ran strong—successful though only in three locations: Manhattan, Boston and northern Vermont. The band also had local gigs in Connecticut, our home state, but we were usually fired in the middle of the first set by distraught club owners.

And so, one might ponder: Why northern Vermont?

During this time a Boston "dancer" named Marlene had joined the band and had moved into the band house, assuming the uninvited role of den mother. Marline, a fearless human, claimed to have been very close to the crew on Jacques Cousteau's ship.

Joe: *What exactly does that mean?*

Marlene: *That's personal!*

For sure, she was perfectly at ease with men, and fit right in with the band, coming up with lyrics for many of our "masterpieces". Marlene was a dark brunet, part French, part Portuguese.

Then we stumbled onto Bunny.

In my state of Connecticut one finds the Pratt & Whitney jet engine manufacturing complex. The work hours there are 7 AM to 3 PM, at which point the gated parking lot is opened and a thousand cars stream out headed for home. Some cars, though, don't go home, and instead drive directly across the street to Club 21 which features "dancers". The place is a money-making gold mine—the big draw: "Bunny".

My band mate Jack, myself and my first wife Janna go to see the Bunny phenomenon. Jack and bass-player Dave had already "scouted" her, so expectations run high. We arrive at 2:30, the place empty, and I introduce the join-the-band, "singing" idea to Bunny, who is immediately interested.

Bunny: *Sounds like a great career move.*

It's a concept thing, really quite brilliant! A power band trio in the middle, with Marlene the brunet on one side and Bunny the blonde on the other. And with punk, singing itself lags second way behind stage presence, so not to worry with these girls.

At 3 PM the flood gates open and half of Pratt & Whitney arrives. Bunny takes center stage, and she isn't just blonde and voluptuous, she is a big performer, a real star. Men throw hundreds of dollars at her within minutes. On her break we organize to pick her up later in the week to attend a band rehearsal so she can gauge the whole operation. If things work out, she can join us in two week's time for a good gig coming up at Yale in New Haven.

Jack and I drive to her housing project, walk up three or four flights of stairs and knock on her door. It opens.

Five guys are staring us down. "What do you want with Bunny?"

I reply. "We have band rehearsal today and she wants to check it out."

"Bunny ain't going."

They step through the door and we start backing down the stairs, flight by flight. More was said by me about giving Bunny a chance, and I thought someone said "We own Bunny." And they probably did. After all it was 2 PM and none of these guys worked. They lived off Bunny.

Now they follow us to the car. We get in. I start the engine, and that's when Jack—as he often did—starts mouthing off to them. In gear, I hit the gas as they chase us down the street.

So much for Bunny.

So we do the New Haven gig with just Marlene—though just to mixed Connecticut reviews. We are comforted only by a *return* engagement gig we have the very next weekend at a sizable club in northern Vermont. That winter, we played numerous dates up north and like said, they actually loved us. So this return gig would make up for Yale. Note: I think the band *Meatloaf* came from up there, so that might be a clue as to our artic draw.

For example, earlier that winter in December, a Montpellier Vt. gig near a college went so well that after the Thursday night show the whole entertainment-starved school turned out for the Friday and Saturday night events. This post-New Haven gig was even further north in the deep woods just miles from Canada. At that moment the dead of winter covered the earth with temperatures of 25 below zero, but as this was our second time there we were ready.

For instance, in the town diner, if you ordered a BLT, it came on untoasted white bread.

Not this second time. I made sure they toasted it. Also, each morning no one's car started, so two guys in a truck drove around with a massive voltage apparatus that caused your car to either start or explode. They got $1 per jump. This was the life.

Ok, it's Thursday night. We set up in the band room, which has around 20 tables. Next to this is the "club's" entry foyer, and across this, a large standing-only bar room which accommodates many more.

All of the patrons are lumber jacks.

So far they have been in the woods all week, the warmest day reaching negative 7 degrees. These guys are super ready, plus Marlene is back! What an amazing intersection of ingredients for a blow-out weekend!

Time for me to introduce Bear.

To start, Bear always got the center table 3 feet from Marlene. He was the Paul Bunyan of the region. Everybody took direction from him. The "Bear" name stuck easily, as he looked like a bear, had long hair and an endless beard, his large, overweight body and face capped off by a gigantic flat nose, broken years ago through regular brawling in the woods and at the bar. He gives Marlene a big Bear hug and smells her hair.

Joe: *Well Bear, we're back!*

Bear: *Big crowds, big crowds.*

And there were big crowds, though by performing in the band room, I could barely tell what the bar room scene was like, but the foyer area was packed as well so Bear was right—capacity crowds had gathered from all points along this distant frontier.

Marlene was in high gear. She could talk to an audience like a pro stand up comedian. All kinds of nonsense between songs. Bear was so proud of her, and he sat there like a school boy in love.

Friday night more of the same, and then came Saturday, with Bear still sitting close. We performed our original punk material, repeating it three times a night. Bear's favorite, Marlene's autobiographical: LOST VIRGINITY.

Around midnight on Saturday, a commotion erupts over in the bar room, and two guys push through the foyer towards Bear's table to fetch him. We stop playing. I sense danger, put my guitar down, and to get closer to the door, I work my way behind Bear's wake to the foyer area. Against the back wall in the bar room stands a guy waving a large hand gun at the crowd. Three state troopers stand there holding the fort, trying to talk him down.

Like the Red Sea, a path miraculously opens and Bear walks through. The troopers part. Bear walks up to the young gun slinger and holds his hand out to receive the gun. The young man is in tears and simply cries out 'oh Bear" and hands the gun over. Bear takes him into a bear hug to comfort him, and then the fellow is cuffed. Frontier justice!

By 12:30 AM the side show is over; we play one more set until closing.

And that's all I've got to say about that.

Punk Rock Hall of Fame — Lyrics by Marlene

Gonna get my name in the punk rock hall of fame
Pictures and a twist of reality, they'll read about me.

1974
JAMES COTTON

The various eruptions of American musical forms all seem to have come out of nowhere. One-day Rock & Roll does not exist and a year later Chuck Berry and Elvis Presley suddenly dominate Western culture.

The same goes for the Blues. Before "the Blues". poor blacks sang slave chants and spirituals until suddenly some guys from Mississippi invent a unique pattern of chord progressions and snap-shot-like lyrics, all propelled by pulsating guitars and harmonicas. Move over Mozart!

This particular blues eruption takes place amongst a bunch of cats who happen to know each other, all born in the Mississippi delta region between 1910 and 1935. One of the last to be born,

James Cotton, in 1935, reigns even during my era, dying not until 2017.

My encounter with James takes place in 1974.

Back then, in 1974, a nightclub called The Shaboo Inn sits in the middle of empty farmland in Eastern Connecticut.

The Shaboo, a rambling structure made of wood, holding 1,000 + people, attracts the best bands in the world plus armies of baby boomers gladly travelling dark country roads to see them perform.

I find myself there. Sometimes my band opens for a headliner like *Quicksilver Messenger Service* or *Roger McQuinn* of *The Byrd's (photo)*, and sometimes I mindlessly journey there with my bandmates to catch an upcoming act like *The Cars* or *Elvis Costello*. The *James Cotton Band* plays quite often, and I become a big fan.

The Ramones at Shaboo

Back in the 1950's James, being a relative Blues youngster, is mentored by many of his Mississippi predecessors as a side man in their bands, just as James himself described in the last lyric he wrote before his death:

> *I learned from Sonny Boy*
> *Him and Howlin' Wolf too*
> *Twelve years with Muddy Waters*
> *And I know what I had to do ...*
> *Father Time has slipped up on me*
> *Long gone is my youth*
> *I look in the mirror each morning*
> *And I'm staring at the truth.*

(Photo: James, singing with B.B. and Muddy)

(James, Johnny & Muddy)

But James is not just the caboose on the end of the blues foundation train, he is the link between those old blues masters and the more recent blues champions like Johnny Winter, Mike Bloomfield, Janis Joplin, Buddy Guy, Jimmie Hendrix, Bonnie Raitt and Eric Clapton. Hence he is a very big deal as both a player and an icon.

Which brings us to the encounter.

After seeing James at The Shaboo a handful of times, playing to packed audiences, I go again on a Tuesday night and find the place is empty.

Actually totally empty. Me and a couple of friends sit on the wood floor right in front of the band with no one else in attendance.

To my total amazement, this absence of an audience does not phase these guys at all. They are on fire, fully engaged as entertainers with just us. The drummer is all energy, the bass player hammers his fretless electric bass, *Matt "Guitar" Murphy* (photo) shines and James... well with James, every note, every vocal phrase, every comedy look is delivered as if he were on stage at Woodstock.

Then they take a break.

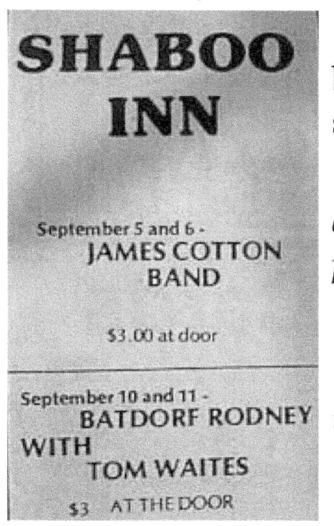

Don't know where the band went, but James just stands off to the side all sweated up, so I go over to say hello.

Hey James, saw you here a month ago and I couldn't move, must've been 1,500 people. What happened?

Tuesday? Who knows.

Really appreciate you guys going all out tonight.

Why not? Like to play.

J.A. PATRINA

Right then a girl comes up to us. She is Ellen, my sister's best friend, who must have been sitting in the bar room during the first set.

Ellen, completely ignoring James Cotton: *Joey, how you doing. How's the band? You playing here again soon? The last time I saw you the band smoked.*

Joe: *Ah Ellen say hello to James. Know who he is?*

Ellen: *Yea the harmonica player.*

I smirk at James. He gets a kick out of the scene.

Photo: Mark Knopfler at Shaboo

James: *Glad to meet you Ellen.*

Want some popcorn? Ellen offers.

James, smiling: *No thanks. It will plug up my harmonica.*

Joe: *Ellen, James here is one of the most important blues guys in the world.*

Ellen: *Oh!!! Didn't know.*

Joe: *We're lucky to have him. Years ago in Chicago, James was shot in the back and survived.*

James: *Shot eight times.*

Photo: Lou Reed at The Shaboo

Ellen doubting this: *And lived?*

Joe: *James show her the evidence.*

James pulls up the back of his sweat-drenched shirt and one can see the bullet welts on his back.

Joe: *See, I told you we're lucky to have him.*

James pulls down his shirt and looks around for his band, Ellen leaves.

Pausing another moment, he looks at me and says: *And now son, you know why we come out to do our best, every show. Could be the last one. Hope you like the second set.*

Joe: Just do Rocket 88 and it'll be great.

James: *Will do.*

And it was so.

My favorite Cotton lyric: *"What I say to make you mad this time BA-BY?"*

P.S. Years later The Shaboo Inn burnt down, allegedly torched for insurance money. Regardless, it meant the end of an era, great bands rising out of nowhere playing to baby boomers in organic settings. Arena rock followed.

And that's all I've got to say about that.

1979
SOL GOLDMAN

Before Donald Trump dominated New York real estate there was Sol Goldman, the 600-buildings tycoon who rented me one room... and it helped me to climb up.

New York real estate is the most amazing thing. It never goes down. Big money earners swarm in from all points and wealthy families from civilized and brutal countries alike park wealth in the Big Apple causing perpetual demand for ridiculously tiny spaces. Everyone knows this.

After I graduated from Trinity College, and then worked for GFOX and the State of Connecticut, my next break surfaced with Jimmy Carter's CETA program—the Comprehensive Education Training Act. Rather than permanent welfare, CETA provided money to get the un- or underemployed trained in something of value, so they might actually survive long term without government monies.

All my friends signed up, but for the dopiest of job training jobs, like raking leaves in the park.

One program held real promise: a one-year immersion into computer programming combined with internships in actual Hartford corporations like the gigantic Aetna and Hartford Fire insurance companies. By signing up for this program, my future became possible, though it meant one more year in Hartford.

I discover that software is like music: unbelievably creative and intricate, but with no mistakes tolerable. Next step: get a job.

First I go to Boston. But Boston seems just a bigger Hartford, and after my New York experiences, including Punk Rock, I said "screw it", and decide to interview in New York.

While interviewing, my wife Janna, on Chemotherapy up in Hartford, stays with her parents. In New York, I crash at a $6 a night flop house on West 36th Street filled with ex-cons and washed up boxers. It is July, 100 degrees even at night, as Manhattan's concrete never cools down; there are no locks, just beds to the door, bedbugs and communal showers.

With this as "home-sweet-home", I put my GFOX blue suit on each morning, float between midtown and Wall Street and interview. I accept a programming position at The Bank of New York, the bank started by Alexander Hamilton.

Ok, so The Bank of New York is a go. But what about an apartment? I gravitate to the upper east side, walk the streets, and at one point see a man hosing down the sidewalk on 81st street. He is the "super", a Hungarian named Rocky, the building's resident janitor, living in the basement.

Rocky says a "rent controlled" studio apartment is just coming free but I need to talk to the owner over at Solil Management in mid-town.

I immediately walk to mid-town, find the Solil building, find the rental office, fill out the application and tell the receptionist to please let someone look at it right away as I did not want the apartment to slip through my fingers. I would wait.

Time passes and a woman comes out to tell me that because I just got the job at Bank of New York—and had no other meaningful employment history or guarantors—that Solil could not rent me the $400 a month apartment against my $18,000 <u>future</u> salary.

I make my case: Educated at Trinity College, a 3.75 average in International Economics, cross trained in Data Processing at top Hartford Insurance Companies. I had received a dozen job offers, had never let anyone down, ever, and …

Right then a voice from an adjoining room said: *Jane, bring him in to me.*

He introduced himself as Sol Goldman (I did not realize what this meant).

Tell me which of these job offers you accepted?

The Bank of New York.

Why?

Alexander Hamilton.

Go on.

He founded the bank, the first bank in America. At 26, he was Washington's general in the battle of New York. He came here with nothing and I want to work there.

Why?

To build courage.

Jane, give the man the apartment.

Later I found that Sol was self-made, married to Lillian, their business called Solil. Upon his death in 1987, when I still dwelled in the one room, Jane, his daughter, sued her mother, wrestling 2/3 of the assets from the mother. Ah… New York real estate.

Also, while working at The Bank of New York, at lunch I brought 30 programmers over to the bank's executive office on 44 Wall Street to see the board room, furnished, I had read, by Hamilton himself. Our V.P. was shocked when security called saying a bunch of us with valid company IDs wanted access. The bank president's secretary gave us a tour.

Years later, after founding Wall Street Systems, The Bank of New York became my customer, and when their data center burned down on 9/11 inside #7 World Trade, a long attachment made me a committed participant in the bank's complicated disaster recovery effort involving all of their major systems.

And that's all I've got to say about that.

1981
MADONNA

Of all the self-made people I met along the way, none outdid "self-made" more than Madonna, even to the extent of creating her own name. She would point this out to me during our encounter.

After moving to New York City in 1979—while endlessly designing software for the bank and navigating the throws of my first wife's cancer fight—I nevertheless remained fully engaged in music. Members of my 1970's punk band had moved to the city, so musicians were readily available and

music rehearsal spaces rented by the hour all made it easy to organize a three-hour jam. *Photo, a NYC rehearsal room.*

For instance, on Broadway, near the theaters, a whole building exists for rehearsing musical theater productions.

For rock, on west 29th Street we frequented a music complex housing around 20 small studios, each with a built-in vocal sound system, a keyboard, amplifiers and drum kit, going for $20 an hour. You brought your own guitars.

But our favorite was Albert Crabtree's' space on 36th Street, west of 8th Avenue, next to the Port Authority Bus Station (kidnapping central), deep in the pimp, peep show and pornography district. And as it would be a decade before this 42nd Street sewage was cleaned up by Rudy Gulianni. We certainly caught the grime wave first hand. *Photo: 42nd Street, 1980*

One found Crabtree's' studio up a freight elevator on the tenth floor of an industrial building built around 1900. I never could figure who rented all the other floors, as no directory appeared, I only know that on the ground floor a fake delicatessen operated fronting a drug selling operation. Transvestites prowled outside the "deli" trying to trick naïve Johns. Most people would shudder at all this, but to some, it was musician heaven.

Besides residing in a great neighborhood, the studio's accoutrements were perfect: a 40-by-40-foot performance space with high ceilings and a one-foot, step-up stage looking out onto a scattering of couches. Behind this couch area, mounted in the room's rear wall, a recording studio window beaconed—should one be ready to record.

The performance space was circled by a corridor. Across the corridor, 15 dark, curtained, little "monk" hutches were occupied by musicians who slept in sleeping bags, paying peanuts in rent while enduring endless assaults of hard rock music pounding through the walls. Plus, there was the recording studio control room, and Albert's "office" where people could hang out. The place was happening!

Lots of people came in and out at all hours of the night, the later past midnight the better, and when the elevator doors opened on the tenth floor anyone could be standing there— heavy metal, big hair "shredder" guitarists, Billy Idol (who really looked like Billy Idol at all times), and many others seeped in the world of rock music.

One day as I exit the elevator a brown-haired girl with gorgeous eyes stands in front of me. She steps into the elevator and we nod to each other as the doors close. She disappears.

In the foyer I ask some hangers out: *Who's that?*

Madonna.

Madonna, huh. What does she do?

She sings and dances, and f---s Latinos.

How do you know that?

She just told us. That's where she's going now.

Oh.

I learned that Madonna indeed devoured Latinos, including them in her lifestyle and later in her videos. And long before hooking up with *A Rod* (Alex Rodrigues of the Yankees), she would troll avenues A, B and C on the lower east side looking for interesting targets in that Latin ghetto. This was no feminist; this was a big time adventurer afraid of nothing.

A month later I am in the foyer waiting for the elevator and this time she steps off. I stay put.

Hello we met here a few weeks ago, moving in the opposite directions. You're Madonna right?

Right.

What's your last name?

Just Madonna, I named myself. And you?

I'm Joe, ya know "from birth".

Joe from birth huh? You're going with that?

With a warm smile she adds:

Well maybe you should consider a change.

Madonna in 1982 — going blond

I nod. She waves, and walks away.

Madonna went on to become a mega star, I stayed as "Joe".

Twenty-five years later Madonna buys three townhouses on East 81st Street in New York City, right across from my Penthouse apartment. For months, from our own 16th floor balcony, my family watches as workers turn Madonna's three adjacent buildings into a gigantic $50 million palace set in the midst of Manhattan's Upper East Side.

She had just separated from her English husband and broken off with *A Rod*, and so Madonna moved in with just her gaggle of adopted kids. On Halloween, my kids ring Madonna's doorbell and for treats they get non-carb, non-sugar something's that the cook had dreamed up. You see, everything is done Madonna's way.

And that's all I've got to say about that!

1982
JAKE LAMOTTA

"Ray, you never knocked me down", said by Jake LaMotta to Sugar Ray Leonard after their sixth fight. More on this later. But for now, lets learn about Jake, *The Raging Bull*, who I encountered in Little Italy, New York back in 1982.

When I was young, from the 50's to the 80's, boxing was big, but changing. Fighters fought less and less, with growing gaps of time left between bouts in order to train for the next fight. This clearly contrasted with the pre-WW II era, where one trained for next week's fight with last week's fight.

Jake, born to the Italian Bronx of 1922, used to fight almost daily as a kid. To pay the rent, his father organized neighborhood fist fights between boys, where onlookers would throw coins into "the ring". It was here that Jake learned not to resist a landed punch; just let the head roll away on impact. And when taking a blow straight on without a roll away move, not to give a damn, take the pain, stay on your opponent, bully him, pummel him.

Jake, who lived to 95-years old, turned pro in 1941, at age 19. His first eleven fights took place between May 3 & 14, April 1, 8, 15, 22 & 26, May 20 & 27, and June 9, 18 & 23.

This winning pace continued until he finally lost a match in September. Jake had 106 pro fights in the 1940's and into the early 50's—and was only knocked down once—and not by his nemesis Sugar Ray Robinson!

In any writing about Jake, Sugar Ray needs a few lines written as well. After all, many consider Sugar Ray Robinson the greatest fighter of all time across weight classes. Ray could brawl, Ray could dance, Ray could jab and counterpunch ... Ray created whatever the circumstances called for. *Photo: Jake & Ray at it again.*

Ray had 200 professional bouts, with many of his 18 losses coming only late in his career, once past his boxer's "sell by" date. Ray died at 67, financially broke. But Ray did have one loss that came early on. In the first ten years of boxing, Ray realized over 100 wins, with his *only* loss coming in 1943; it was at the hands of one Jake LaMotta.

After that they fought five more times, with Sugar Ray prevailing thereafter, their last match in 1951. Once past the 11th round, Jake begins to get pummeled by Ray, unable to raise his arm to defend himself. Blow upon blow lands, a punishment beyond comprehension in today's boxing world, until finally the referee stops the fight in the 13th. You can watch it on YouTube.

It was after this match that a defiant LaMotta nevertheless asserts "Ray, you never knocked me down". You see, Jake had knocked Ray down in previous fights, which for Jake meant that he was tougher, regardless of the win/lose numbers.

The Raging Bull movie came out in 1980. Robert Di Nero won an Oscar playing Jake, though the real star for every male viewer was Rita Moreno.

Through the movie I learned that after boxing, Jake decided to become a comedian, and spent decades pursuing this. For example, in referring to a fellow boxer, Jake would say: "He was a very colorful fighter … he bled all over the place." Jake, who bruised (right) but did not bleed, was terrible at comedy, but like boxing, nothing was going to stop him.

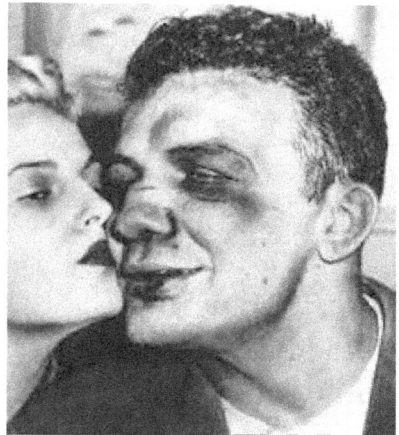

He even started a nightclub in Miami, and people went. Really a 'wise guy', not a comedian, Jake also acted in a number of Hollywood movies as a bit actor. He had friends. He enjoyed life. He made it 95 years

This brings us to the encounter.

It was 1982, I had seen the Raging Bull movie in 1980, and a year prior in 1979, having arrived in NYC looking for a job, I had stayed in a $6-a-night flop house on west 36th Street, filled with old boxers waiting out their days with no place else to go.

J.A. PATRINA

As it happened, my great uncle Vincent Marshall had put time into the same west 36th street "sanctuary" back in the day, before he tamed his drinking. He came from this neighborhood, an Irish ghetto called "Hells Kitchen" (Above). I guess in some way you could say it was my neighborhood too.

These old timer boxers all had a certain look. For one, after being hit in the face thousands of times, their skin appeared "puffy" which helped to blend their broken noses into the rest of the face. But second, they all had a look in their eye. They might be on skid row now, but once upon a time they went toe-to-toe against other warriors, laying bare untold levels of bravery and will. Somehow, even years later, this knightly nobility stayed put within their countenance.

Jake age 60, in 1982

My point? I admire boxers, Jake being one of the bravest knights ever to enter the jousting lists. But the forgotten flophouse guys I met deserve respect as well, just for getting in the ring.

On a beautiful 1982 Sunday morning, my wife Janna and I ride down the subway line headed for our midday lunch at Umberto's Clam House on Mulberry Street, the same restaurant already mentioned in the Abbie Hoffman encounter, the restaurant Joey Gallo was gunned down in. We are early, so we get off the train at Spring Street, and decide to tool around that neighborhood before cutting east over to Little Italy proper. I say "proper" because in the early 1900's the whole area was Little Italy, not just today's Mulberry Street, the remnant that everyone thinks of.

My Italian grandfather Nick, for instance, came out of Spring Street, west of Broadway. In some way it's kinda my neighborhood.

So we are tooling around and on a secondary street we come across a Bocce Court with four old guys playing and a photographer clicking away. One of the old guys has that look: puffy, no nose, and a glean in the eye.

Joe to photographer: *What's happening?*

Photographer: *A promo shoot.*

Joe: *Who's the tough guy?*

Photographer: *That's Jake LaMotta*

What luck! Janna and I stand leaning against the fence separating the Bocce Court from the sidewalk and watch for a while. I am right next to Jake's beaming energy, radiating from his unabashed belief in himself. He gives me a winning look. I take the invite.

Joe: *Jake, you like Bocce?*

Jake: *Na, it's a promo.*

Joe: *Know where you're going to lunch?*

Jake: *We* (pointing to his friends) *haven't talked yet, but I'm thinking about it. How about you and the misses?*

Joe: *We're on our way to Umberto's.*

Jake (chuckling): *Umberto's huh ... well don't get shot!*

You see, he made one of his jokes (Joey Gallo—get it?), and we all actually laughed at it.

And that's all I've got to say about that.

Below: Mauling an opponent

Geeze!

1986
BIG GUY

In 1980, six months into NYC, European American Bank (EAB) offers me a dream job. With my international economics background. I aspire to build a foreign exchange trading system for one of the big players, with the goal of—somehow—going into business. EAB adds up.

At the time, in America, EAB's foreign exchange trading volume measures second, only exceeded by Citibank. But more, *EAB is privately held.* Six of the largest banks in Europe own it as a beach head in America, which means that the board can do what it wants, not beholden to retail or institutional stock holders. Still young (26), I sense that the bank might someday become volatile, as the board seats English, German, French, Belgian, Dutch and Austrian members, and their people already have 2,000 years of fighting under their belts.

This proves the case. After board meetings, gossip trickles down from the Vice Chairmen, to the Executive Vice Presidents, to the Senior Vice Presidents to the mere Vice

Presidents and finally to me, an Assistant Vice President. These reports of boardroom strife give me hope, and I put 12-hour days in for years, building and enhancing the system I designed and managed, waiting for my chance, patience a virtue.

During these years my wife Janna dwells in and out of hospitals receiving the latest concoction of "game changing" chemotherapy. I leave the bank at six, spend time at the hospital, and then work on the phone with Jeff, my design partner, until 1 am, figuring out micro elements for the next day's programming assignments.

Finally, it happens, the bank loses money, and after a huge fight on who to blame, Amsterdam Rotterdam Bank (one of the six) says it will buy the other banks out. They bring in a new CEO to clean house, and around 50 executives are terminated, including my boss *Lucien Kneip* who eventually founds Wall Street Systems with me. I survive due to my junior rank and my nuts and bolts knowledge of much of the bank's operation.

The new CEO is something else! Born in Yonkers, living in Great Neck, L.I., he admits to loving golf, girls and parties, and brags he can get along for weeks on just three hours sleep a night. He regularly holds cocktail parties for us "Bank Officers" telling us these personal things, plus making faux management proclamations, like his plan to reduce office and cubicle sizes, so he can pass the savings on to us, the "officers".

Basically, he wants to squeeze the stuffing out of the bank's expenses and targets whole departments and other things that annoy him.

For example, the bank has two charters originally set up for different business practices, and hence, he has to look at two sets of balance sheet and income statement numbers to track progress. He orders these legal entities merged. IT consultants determine that every system in the bank needs re-programming to achieve this and the big guy is "pissed".

It dawns on me that the whole thing can be mopped up with one line of code.

Each day the departmental systems send journal entries from both companies, #1 & #2, to the general ledger system. Submitted files all run through a "proof check" program to assure each department's debits and credits balance before posting to the official books. My idea is to have the proof check program—the bank-wide pinch point—change incoming company #2 records to be company #1 records so that all entries post to company #1 accounts on the main ledgers.

Leave all of the departmental systems untouched. Pretend that only company #1 exists.

I call the general ledger programmer, who makes the change in a minute and tests it for me. Next I stop in at the Controller's Office with a graphic to present the solution. Next the Controller brings me to the CEO's office. Next the CEO calls the SVP of Systems and tells him to implement it immediately. The System's head, my new boss, takes it well, as it averts disaster.

Still the boys in IT spend a month in quality control testing this one line of code. The day it went "live" no one noticed. That was the point.

After that, the CEO would grab me in the cafeteria, wanting to know how to do this or that, and I become important, a mystery to the whole executive staff. I start calling him "Big Guy" for some reason, and he always says "don't call me that". But I did anyway, figuring he's from Yonkers.

One day, in the cafeteria, Big Guy wants to talk about getting rid of the bank's vault—not a good sign for a bank—and he wants me on that team. I feel like speaking up.

Joe: So after I mow the lawn and wash the cars what are you going to do with me?

BG: Fire you, like everyone else.

And just like Colonel Kurtz in Apocalypse Now, "he meant it".

Joe: Ok clarity helps. Maybe we can work something out.

The new CFO (Chief Financial Officer) that Big Guy brings in takes a shine to me. He loves my trading system and is interested in expanding it beyond foreign exchange to bond sales. I aspire to become his new BFF (duh). He is a southerner from a Florida bank, new to New York, and he explains that where he comes from everyone has normal names, like Jones or Smith, but in New York we are all foreigners with funny names like "Joe Patrina".

Next—get this—the new CFO and Big Guy try to buy the bank using outside borrowed money, and I am in on this too. The day their deal is shot down by the board I drink in deep sympathy with them at the Stanhope Hotel on fifth avenue. Big Guy keeps saying: *We came this close!* And he believed it!

Time to strike has arrived. Lucien Kneip, my former boss, and hidden partner, finesses how to pitch the proposal to get the system.

The deal: we get the system, maintain it for EA3, and get paid as outside contractors to build out the bond sales sub-system for the new CFO—as long as we do no outside business for 18 months.

I call it "The Indentured Servant" agreement.

At one of the cocktail parties before the contract is signed, Big Guy charges over surrounded by other suits and starts cursing saying I am "gonna double cross him".

BG: I'll f...ing kill you. We have budgets for that don't we? he asks the controller, who shakes his head "yes".

Joe: *Big guy...*

BG: *I said not to call me Big Guy.*

Joe: *Ok Big Guy, but how can I double cross you? If you're not happy for the next 18 months I lose everything, plus did I ever let you down?*

BG: *Not yet. Just don't get stupid on me.*

Joe: *It's like I said in the cafeteria, I'll do whatever you need, clean the windows, vacuum the cars, even get the beach sand out of the carpets. You name it. Ya can't lose Big Guy.*

A few years later after EAB is sold to Citi Bank and Wall Street Systems is off and running, I run into Big Guy at a restaurant, go over to say hi, commenting that all of his rough stuff really paid off (he had just gotten a huge bonus). His wife says that since then "he's been a sweetheart", which led me to say:

Ok, so I'll drop Big Guy. from now on, you're Sweetheart.

I can still see his big smile, waving his finger "no".

And that's all I have to say about that.

1980
REGGIE JACKSON

People are amazed when I say I am both a New York Yankee and a Boston Red Sox fan. How could this be?

In 1952 while my father was at sea, I was born at a Navy hospital in Queens, New York. After first living in Queens we moved to Long Island, living there through the 1950s and into the early 1960s, right when the Yankees were the greatest team on earth. So that explains that.

Soon thereafter the Yankees effectively fell off a cliff, right when the Red Sox came alive and right when my family moved north to Connecticut. One could not watch Carl Yastrzemski, Tony Conigliaro and Carlton Fisk without becoming a fan.

After the Red Sox had their hey day, in 1979 I moved back to New York to launch my career, and guess what? Led by the boss, George Steinbrenner, managed by Billy martin and Yogi Berra, and featuring amazing players like Catfish Hunter, Ricky Henderson and Reggie Jackson, the Yankees rose to the top once more (Steinbrenner and Reggie).

Reggie lived in my neighborhood, ate at the same Greek coffee shop—Nectar on Madison at 79th Street—and had his signed picture sitting above the coffee shop grill. But this did not form the basis for my admiration of him. His playing did. Plus, back then he carried a gun, saying he was always being hassled.

His handle "Mr. October" did not refer to just one fabulous stint of hitting during one October world series season, but to all of the Octobers he participated in, hauling in 18 home runs in playoff games, and 10 more during world series games.

The peak of it all took place in game 6 of the 1977 world series when Reggie hit three home runs off three different pitchers and pitch types: fastball, curve and change up.

In 1980 I went to or watched every Yankee game either at the stadium or on WPIX New York. If they were in California, I stayed up late. It got so that I knew who was going to hit that day and if pitchers had their stuff. To witness Reggie's 400th home run, I went to five straight games, sitting in the $4.50 grandstand seats a little towards third, so I could peer into the Yankee dugout—in case Reggie had another fight with Billy Martin—but no fights or home runs surfaced.

The next day after each of those five games Reggie would be at Nectar having breakfast and I never said nothing. First I followed the New Yorker code to leave celebrities alone, and second, I always remembered, he carried a gun. I had to witness number 44 hit number 400 watching TV.

Back then Reggie was gigantic. I am broad shouldered, but his shoulders and chest torso dwarfed me and every other human I ever saw, including Mike Tyson. One day he walks into Nectar wearing a white t-shirt and crisp blue overalls that make him look even bigger. He sits one table away across from me and for once I keep looking up to see if what I just saw is real. Finally, he reacts.

Stop looking at me when I'm eatin' my eggs! He demands staring me down.

Reggie, I reply, *I'm here every day and I and everyone else always leave you alone. It's just that I've never seen overalls in Manhattan before.*

I'm a spokesman for Murjani Jeans now. I have to wear them.

Until then, the two big spokespeople for Murjani were Debra Harry of Blondie and Gloria Vanderbilt, so in someone's mind, Reggie was perfect for the job. Can't you see this?

Well if you're trying to advertise those overalls you're doing great, I say with a warm smile and wave it off, both of us going back to our eggs.

The next day he arrives without the overalls, gives me a look and he never wore the overalls again. Murjani—out of Israel—went out of business at some point after Gilder Radner made fun of the brand, doing her Jewish Jeans bit, with big hair and oversized sun glasses. "Jewish Jeans—guaranteed to ride up."

Twenty-five years later, in say 2005, my second wife Laura and I are in an empty Nectar at 11:00 am sitting at the same table I occupied during the Murjani incident, and a Mercedes sedan pulls up outside. A driver gets out, opens the passenger door and Reggie steps out with a lot less hair then he once had, his shoulders now only as wide as mine, and he steps inside, going to the counter to order a coffee to go—probably for old times sake.

He turns to leave and sees me, does a double take, not knowing where this *Deja Vous* moment came from, and I wave. He nods back.

Best of all for me, a few years later Reggie re-joined the Yankees as a player-mentor figure. The man has a big heart and he followed it back to New York.

Jeter & Reggie

And that's all I've got to say about that.

Career home runs:

Mickey Mantel: 536

Reggie Jackson: 563

Alex Rodriguez: 696

Babe Ruth: 714

1989
CLAUS PESHEK

It's 1989, my partner Lucien and I just signed a contract with European American Bank (EAB) assigning the rights to the bank's *Foreign Exchange* Trading software to our new company, Wall Street Systems. Plus, separately, we won an $1.8 million consulting contract to build out a *bond* trading system for the new EAB Chief Financial Officer. Soon, we needed to launch ourselves out into the market, before our $1.8 million dried up.

We had friends at two of the New York branches of Deutsche Bank and what was to become Bank Austria. Both of these gigantic banks had once owned shares in European American Bank before Amsterdam Rotterdam bought them out. Our New York friends, though, were in no position to purchase a major trading platform like ours. This kind of decision would need to be approved by their respective headquarters in Frankfurt and Vienna.

Bank Austria

As big a deal as Deutsche Bank was and is, in 1989 the top guy at Bank Austria, Claus Peshek, was legendary in the foreign exchange world. You might not remember this, but after World War II Austria was kept "on ice" by the Allies, including Russia, until 1955, held without permission to establish a national currency.

My sense of the period was that the West wanted Austria free, and the Russians wanted to fold it into the Soviet constellation, like East Germany, Poland, Hungry, et. al.

In 1955, the West won the square off with Stalin (Stalin died in '53), and now it was time to make Austria a working country with a viable currency—the Austrian Schilling. (below American, British, French and Soviet officers on Austria liberation day in 1955).

A brilliant young man named Claus Peshek was tapped to achieve a smooth introduction of the Austrian Schilling into the world

markets in a manner where no panic buying or selling would take place.

Claus established a real economic basis for the Shilling's intrinsic worth, and convinced the leading European banks to respect this starting exchange rate. Peshek succeeded with this in 1955, and hence in 1989, when I met him, he was still legendary.

And so, if Peshek wanted to hire Wall Street Systems, we would be off and running.

That June, the 1989 foreign exchange convention "FOREX" was taking place in Honolulu Hawaii. Everyone was going, especially the big shots in Europe who wouldn't miss it for anything. So the plan was for us partners of Wall Street Systems (Joe, Lucien and Jeff) to buy a 10-by-10 space on the FOREX Trade Show floor at Hilton Hawaiian Villages, and have our New York friends steer the big shots (Peshek) our way.

It worked! Here's how.

This was before flat screen TVs, so we rent a giant tube screen and fly it out to Honolulu. We place a long folding table in front of our colorful ten-foot display unit, blocking the entrance into the display area. We sit the big TV on this table facing out, and place two chairs in front of the screen. These jut out onto the Trade Show floor, making people walking by to step around them.

Other vendors come by feeling sorry for us, saying the TV should be inside the display area so we can invite people in, not keep people out. "The table is blocking the flow".

And besides, if I get a prospect to look at the system on the TV, my back will be to the convention hall, keeping me from making eye contact with other candidates. I was doing it all wrong.

Us vendors had plenty of time to chat like this while waiting for conference attendees who were in seminars until 3 PM each day.

But for three days running, at 3 PM, rather than strolling through the trade show area, all of the FOREX traders quickly escaped to the beach. No one came by. One of the vendors was REUTERS, who had a huge $ million dollar display unit dominating the hall, with around 20 sales people, including beautiful women. Our tiny display unit cost $ 10,000. Either way, no one came by.

Finally, on the last day, the conference leaders spoke to the attendees, and at 3 PM—following a speech by the U.S. Treasury Secretary—dutifully, they all swarmed into the trade show hall by the hundreds.

Our Bank Austria friend comes over saying he spoke to Peshek, who is coming in to find us, saying:

Pesheck is around 5' 7'', with hair brushed strait back, sporting a classic Viennese goatee.

Next a 6' 6'' German steps up. He is Gerhard Steskal, the head dealer from Deutsche Bank, and my partner Lucien engages him in conversation. Gerhard would have been a Panzer Division colonel during the war. Later, once he became a prized customer, I would watch in awe as he directed his whole trading operation using his voice and physical presence to "move the market", trading billions in just minutes, using buy/sell tactics designed for the bank's self-interest.

Then I spot Peshek, wearing a Hawaiian bathing suit and matching top, saying hello to everyone near him, while looking all over the place for his assigned destination—me. I go out and fetch him.

Mr. Peshek, it's Joe Patrina from Wall Street Systems, thanks for stopping by.

I'm supposed to see Wall Street.

We're all ready for you. Sit here and I'll give you the low down on what it's all about.

Claus sits, and suddenly 80 foreign exchange dealers rush over to see what the great Peshek is up to. A wide arc of onlookers forms, with Lucien and Gerhard, the Deutsche Bank head trader, standing behind me.

Now I happened to know that Peshek had been a Vienna Boys Choir member in his youth and that his wife was an opera singer, so, as you will see, I quickly incorporated music into the presentation. Peshek says for me to call him Claus. I begin.

Well Claus, to start, we rented this TV screen, but the computer running it is in our data center in New York. You can plug in from anywhere. In your case the computer would be in Vienna, and Vienna, London, New York, Hong Kong trading rooms, and other minor branches would all trade off the single platform. And you personally could be anywhere on earth, log in, and get a snap shot of your world-wide operation.

He stares at me, amazed. I proceed.

But though global in architecture, the system's micro features are designed to flow with the step-by-step mental processes of the individual trader. Each trader configures their screen for the type of trading they do: dollar based, currency pair based, FX Interest Arbitrage based, etc.

I then run through a few trading exercises, and then show him how easy it is to find information, saying how carefully we built it, all by working with the traders at our old bank — European American, where he had been a member of the board. Then I say:

With software everything needs to be perfect, like music.

Like music, he interjects.

Exactly like music, the composition needs to be balanced and arranged, and every note counts. Bad notes crash a symphony orchestra, and with software bad notes crash the system. But once you get it perfect, it's perfect, like printing records of a great performance.

How do you know so much about music?

Myself and Jeff (standing nearby) *are both serious musicians, and we took to software like fish in a pond.*

I look over my shoulder at Jeff, and for the first time, gauge the size of the mob gathered behind me. Through the cracks

I see the Reuter's people across the hall, starring at us, no one visiting them. Claus gets up and begins to speak in German to Gerhard the Deutsche Bank guy, not realizing that my partner Lucien speaks fluent French and German. Translated:

Claus: *This looks great, are you going to buy it.*

Gerhard: *We want to, but not on our own.*

Claus: *Well not on our own either, but if you go, we'll go with you.*

They both sign up.

And for the next few years I spend a lot of time in Vienna, with Armin Steppan, the powerhouse forex trader temporarily taken off the Bank Austria desk to implement the system with me and my team. Armin and I, who became the greatest of friends, would work all day in the trading room, and in the evening direct my New York programmers who were building software customizations for the bank.

Then, once a week, at 10 PM, Armin and I would go to Peshek's office. The three of us would cross over to a late-night, fine dining restaurant set upon the old Vienna ring wall, have a perfect meal, plenty of wine, cigars and cognac, and listen to everything Peshek, the great mentor and educator, had to say.

And that's all I've got to say about that.

On the right, the ring wall in the 1800's, protecting "Wien" (Vienna), the capitol of the Austro-Hungarian Empire.

1984
MEMPHIS WARD SCHAEFFER
& THE CABBIES

I think I'm ready to write about Ward ...Ward Schaeffer that is, a guy born in the Appellation Mountains of northern Georgia (think *Deliverance*), later dwelling in Memphis, Tennessee. Ward's the one who showed me songwriting.

Ward, all trouble all the time, a white, boisterous, bearded, big-bellied bulk of a guitar-picking man, raised by black people ... with a red, puffed out, construction worker's pony tail, playing a hollow-bodied Gibson 335 ... Ward was a hillbilly poet who I rallied to, but ultimately could not save.

Considering the above, you can imagine the influence Ward had on my life, but the good didn't stand alone, as he was also an idiot. Though I would try, there was nothing I could do to keep the idiot side from eclipsing the poet.

A year before we met, out in Arizona, Ward, encountered Jack, my lifelong BFF and probably worse trouble than Ward. A lot went down out there that need not be repeated, and these two drifters decided to move back east all the way to New York City to "start fresh", where I happened to be permanently camped out.

It was at a jam session at *Albert Crabtree's* west 36th Street studio that I first encountered Ward. Jack had moved in to one of the studio's "monk beehive" musician cubicles, and Ward was hanging out there one night as myself, Jack, Dave and Jimmy worked out on the performance room stage. As we were *kicking out the jams*, Ward, kept popping his head up in the control room window overlooking us players planted in the performance room.

Finally, Jack, my BFF, explained: That's Ward, the guy I have been travelling with since California. So we meet and say our hello's.

I do not remember the next phase, but it all resulted in Ward joining our Beatnik Rock, NYC scene. Though I truly appreciated his authenticity—him raised by a Black family in Appalachia and all that—I most appreciated that Ward had written 300 songs, many worthy—and so I knew him to be the real deal and not just a vagabond. We started playing, and soon I was fully in his corner, wanting his music to reach America.

Back then, like Carlos Santana, my guitar playing was my voice, though unlike Carlos, my actual vocal abilities later rose to my guitar-speaking capabilities. And so with Ward as the sole vocalist, the guitar work I conjured served strictly as counterpoint to every lyric and emotion uttered by his tortured voice. We were a duet, and I relished each moment of framing and re-stating Ward's lyrical content.

Often, while my wife Janna was in the cancer wards of one of New York's famed research hospitals, the boys, Ward included, would "stay over" at my studio apartment on 81st street in New York, to record music and to expound upon all of the troubles of the world. At daybreak, all accepted sleep on the floor, but sometimes great music had been captured on my dual TEAC four-track recorders, the same machines the Beatles had used on Sargent Pepper.

Dave, on Bass, the equivalent of John Entwhistle of the WHO, and Jimmy, my brother-in-law, a virtuoso drummer and exotic sounds specialist, the equivalent of Brian Enno of KING CRIMSON, and Jack a drummer and vocalist, the equivalent of Johnny Rotten of the SEX PISTOLES were—with me on lead guitar—the backline behind Ward. We were far out. We were Beatnik Rock, our own creation.

Well, though Ward was a perfect buddy while in our midst, don't forget this: Ward was a hillbilly raised by Appellation Blacks. Ward did not fit in anywhere else in America, let alone in Manhattan.

So if we went out, say, for a bite to eat at a coffee shop, our overlooked side of Ward would immediately show itself within polite society, and it was not good. The whole table, and not just Ward, was, let's say, "unwanted" on the upper east side of Manhattan, and for that matter, on the upper east side of the United States.

But so what?

Of all Ward's songs. LOVING YOU was my favorite, a masterpiece of American country brevity. Ward had the knack of saying a lot in very few words, and LOVING YOU was his hallmark, a song where he just could not get over loving a certain girl.

Frankly, I forget which girl the song was written about, as Ward was married six times, but to one of them twice, but that is not the point. Whoever the girl was, Ward loved her without end. Notice the short, clipped verses:

The geese have flown,
even their shadows are gone,
still I'm here loving you.
Loving you. Yes, loving you.
I'm still in love with you.

That New England gloom,
the snows came to soon.
Still I'm here loving you.
Loving you. Yes, loving you.
I'm still in love with you.

Dream our dreams,
they ain't all what they seem.
Still I'm here loving you.
Loving you. Yes, loving you.
I'm still in love with you.

The fire light's bright,
and you're with me tonight.
Still I'm here loving you.
Loving you. Yes, loving you.
I'm still in love with you.

On guitar, I joined with a Chet Atkins rhythmic counterpoint and a beautiful Les Paul-styled guitar solo, and the whole thing was a master piece.

Great, now what? Let's record it.

So Ward agrees, and he finds two backup singers to weigh in on the "Loving You" choruses: Marie, a petite Black girl from Bleecker Street in the Village, and Ud, a burly baritone construction worker from Brooklyn.

We get together at *Duraz's* rehearsal studio on West 28th Street and play the song a few times, flawlessly. But something had gone down and Ward was distraught. He leaves, and goes to an Irish bar called the "Molly We" and gets sauced. Us musicians stay put upstairs in the studio and get to know each other.

Ward surfaces and apologizes. We go down to the street. Ud departs. But Ward, feeling bad, insists on driving us all home, Marie to Bleecker, me and Jimmy to the Upper East Side, and Jack and Dave to the Upper West Side. We say no. Ward insists, and as all of us want closure, we finally say yes.

Inside of Ward's van, parked in front of the 28th street rehearsal studio, is his number one dog Banjo, a black Lab. Banjo would wait forever in the van 'till Ward re-appeared. So we get in with Banjo, throwing ourselves and our guitar cases in the back, giving Marie shotgun. Marie is to be dropped off first, downtown on Bleecker Street.

In the back with Banjo, we can't see anything as Ward cruises seventh avenue south towards Bleecker. I am exhausted, spacing out, but soon snap to, realizing that Ward is in a game of chicken with a bunch of yellow cabs racing down seventh. The violence of breaking hard at red lights is followed by bad language between Ward and the cabbies.

At full speed, Ward, takes a sharp left onto Bleecker, us flying against the side of the van, and after a block or two he slams on the breaks in front of the jazz clubs. A yellow cab crashes into our rear.

I kick open the van's side door, and get out, finding Ward's rear bumper entangled with the lead cab's front bumper, with two other cabs behind this one, all of the drivers stepping out pulling guns. I avoid eye contact.

Marie takes off, Jack and Banjo stay in the van, as Ward starts gunning the engine wanting to escape. Jimmy, Dave and I jump on the twisted bumpers trying to dislodge them as the van surges, until I realize that the coming explosion of metal will amputate our legs, so we jump off, right when the bumpers release, and get this ... we jump back in the van for our guitars, and Ward takes off headed for the Bowery, the three cabs in pursuit.

At Houston and Bowery, Ward slams on the breaks. I kick the doors open again, grab my two guitar cases, and my brother-in-law Jimmy and I hop out, hoping the cabbies leave us be. The holdup is Banjo the dog! He jumps out as well, crying, traumatized, wanting to go with us.

Ward, the hillbilly starts screaming at the dog.

Banjo, you dang dog, get yourself in here, over and over again. Banjo is a wreck. I lift him up to the side entrance and push his butt, getting him inside to join Jack and Dave, and slam the door.

Ward races off, the yellow's following, Jack later reported, down past World Trade. I grab a cab and go home with Jimmy.

Jeeze! Is this what they did in Appalachia?

And that's all I've got to say about that.

PS. Before Ward died, he sold his 335 to me, needing money for his son down in Georgia. Guitar below.

1985
MUHAMMAD ALI

Though I only encountered Muhammad one time in late 1985, his influence on my courage reservoir looms eternal.

Muhammad was ten years older than me, and that doesn't seem like much now. But in 1965 when he twice fought Sonny Liston, I weighed in at age 13, he at 23. Sonny was the scariest guy I had ever seen and, like always, I feared for Muhammad's life. This pattern would repeat for fifteen years—me staring in awe at the TV—wondering how the guy could ignore fear, avoid disaster and prevail.

In the end—from 1978 fighting Spinks until 1980 fighting Larry Holms—I literally cried my eyes out as Ali sacrificed his very brain, going toe to toe, wailing away without defense, horrible...

Above—The early years, when Mohammad still ducked punches.

Besides Ali's boxing history and his Vietnam draft episode, I most try to fathom what went down between young *Muhammad* and *Malcom X* right before *The Nation of Islam* assassinated Malcom in 1965. (Ali and Malcom below)

The "Nation's" founder, *Elijah Muhammad* preached that Blacks should not even try to integrate with whites; just do your Black thing—separate names, separate religion—and deal as equals. Cassius Clay (Muhammad called it his slave name) agreed and upon his ascendency at age 22, he became Muhammad Ali.

Elijah Muhammad, Nation of Islam

In the *Autobiography of Malcom X*, which Malcom was dictating to Alex Haley (*of Roots fame*) right up until the shooting ... Malcom claims that Ali, a fellow Nation of Islam member, shunned Malcom once Malcom called out *Elijah Muhammad* for fathering children out of wedlock.

Anyway, to me, Malcom X and Muhammad Ali showed as much courage as anyone ever could. Malcom died when I was a boy, but my chance to meet Muhammad came around 20 years later.

I owe the encounter to *Sandy* who originally ran administration for our department at the bank. When Lucien and I founded *Wall Street Systems*, Sandy joined us as one of the original nine employees. An old soul indeed, she mentored me in many ways, and even cared for my cancer stricken wife in the final months.

Her personality was so big that when she moved over to Wall Street Systems, everyone thought she was a partner.

Her husband Larry operated various show business ventures and Sandy had met Ali on numerous occasions and talked about him all the time. Another promotional event came up involving Ali, and Larry called saying Muhammad was with him and wanted to see Sandy. She grabs me and says: *Get your coat we're going to see Muhammad at the Plaza (hotel).*

With the Beatles—look how little they are!

On the way she says: *Muhammad knows all about us leaving the bank to go out on our own.*

Joe: *Really?*

Arriving at the Plaza main entrance, many are circling around to get a look at the champ. At 6' 3", you can't miss him, very imposing. Sandy cuts through the crowd with me in tow, walks up to Ali, pokes him in the stomach and says: *Looking a little chubby there, champ!*

He is thrilled to see her, and after some banter I get introduced.

MA: *Sandy told me about you and your wife*

This impresses me to no end. Muhammad might have been told about our little company, but he had obviously picked up where the big human survival battle raged. I tried to be funny.

Joe: *Oh, she told you about that? Well that's 'cause Sandy's the greatest Muhammad, I guess that makes you second greatest.*

MA: *What… I <u>am</u> the greatest on earth!*

With a twinkle in his eye, he directs his sparing move at me and everyone breaks out laughing.

And that's all I've got to say about that.

Know when you are blessed! *Above: Malcom X and Ali in better times.*

1987
HOWARD COSELL

This is my saddest encounter, and I put off writing it for years until friends convinced me to include it both as a telling revelation of my own story and because it reveals Howard's deep nobility. So, it made the book! As always, let's start by saying a few words about Howard before we get to the brief, though heartfelt, encounter.

A Brooklyn NY childhood, a WW II major, a NYU Law School graduate, and perhaps the greatest sports analyst and commentator of all time ... it makes one ponder ... where did America come up with people like this, and is it still possible for our civilization to produce them?

I had no idea of Howard's roots back in the 60's when I first "heard" Howard on TV. Back then, the giants of TV were Walter Cronkite, Johnny Carson and Cosell, the first two forming a type of cultural ballast for us regular citizens.

Howard, though, existed as a force of nature, a de-stabilizer, presiding everywhere, an authority on everything, a guy with a snarl, a chip on his shoulder, a revealer of the fragility of Humankind itself

There! That is how he spoke … regularly, about everybody in and out of sports. In truth, he was a profound critic, an unchallengeable analyzer, a decomposer of the essence of any athlete or luminary caught in his ever-searching rifle scope.

Though despised by some, only an idiot would not want to listen to Howard's pronouncements, with his catch phrase "tell it like it is" acting as cover to justify his outlandish streams of consciousness.

His greatest projects were Muhammed Ali and Monday Night Football—including his announcement to the world that John Lennon had just been murdered. The Muhammed years came first in the 1960's when Mohammed was still Cassius Clay. Howard became the first to accept Clay's new Muhammed Ali name—less Black slave sounding, as you see, Howard had changed his name from Cohen to Cosell—less Jewish sounding. A longstanding bond formed.

Besides trust, Muhammed, perhaps the greatest self-promoter of my lifetime, realized Howard to be his perfect partner, able to tee up situations for Muhammed to react to.

Broadcaster Larry Merchant put it this way: *Before Ali was embargoed from fighting (for refusing military induction), there was a kind of symbiosis in which he and Cosell recognized how they could use each other in a positive way, Ali did not feel threatened by Cosell. And Cosell recognized, as we all did, that there never had been another athlete quite like Ali.*

Monday Night Football

In 1970 Roone Arledge of ABC concocted Monday Night Football with the NFL and tapped Howard to be the show's spark plug. Many viewers complained about putting up with Howard just to watch the game. But the ratings were huge, and this success changed the economic pillars of both the NFL and MLB ever since, leading to today's multi-billion-dollar enterprises.

Finally, there was the death of John Lennon during Monday Night Football, December 8th, 1980. Along with millions, I heard Howard proclaim this stunning news to the world.

And now the 1987 encounter.

In September of '87, my wife Janna lay dying at Mount Saini Hospital in New York. It was her tenth year on Chemotherapy, and the doctors finally gave up, saying she had but a week left to live.

Leading up to this inevitable moment, I had been investigating a Japanese vegetarian diet called *Macrobiotics* that essentially starves cancer cells via greatly reduced levels of glucose (sugar) in the blood stream. I arranged to take Janna home, and hired two cooks who specialized in the diet to come in daily.

The doctor walked us down to the hospital exit, I grabbed a yellow cab and lifted Janna out of the wheel chair and into the car. The doctor asked: *What's next?* and I said I would try the diet. He replied with one of the most twisted statements I ever heard … *It will kill her!*

So, there we are, back in our little studio apartment eating all of this prepared food. A week later she does not die. Soon she gets around the apartment. Eventually she would take cabs to the west side for Macrobiotic cooking lesions.

We are a month in since leaving the hospital, and on a fine October day I suggest we venture out with the wheel chair, and work our way down to the Plaza Hotel, for brunch at the Edwardian Room—green tea and sautéed vegetables. I had just spoken to my mother who did not like the idea, saying that being in public with the wheel chair could backfire. But we had to try.

I admit, walking down Park Avenue I felt alienated. What were people thinking seeing us two pathetic souls?

We make it to 61st Street and I stand at the corner ready to cross, waiting for the lights to change. That's when Howard appears, in a dark blue suit, lit cigar, strolling up to the same corner with another guy who is carefully listening to whatever Howard is going on about. We look at each other.

Across the street, I suddenly see a family from the town Janna and I grew up in. It was Johnny and his parents. Johnny lived in the house adjacent to Janna's and they had been childhood friends. In recent years Johnny was getting work on TV, and great expectations held that he would soon become a star. Janna and I were pumped to see them, and rather than cross, we stood still to greet them as they arrived on our side of the street.

Walking towards us, though, I sensed something amiss in their countenances, and sure enough, as the got close, they coolly nodded, put an arm around Johnny their budding star and hurried on by us.

Janna and I stood crestfallen. And then it happened. I felt a touch on my shoulder. Turning and looking up at the 6' 3" Cosell, he simply said:

I'm very sorry for what I just saw.

And that's all I've got to say about that.

P.S. Johnny fizzled out.

That's Muhammed peaking under Howard's toupee.

Janna eventually gave up, went off the diet and chained smoked Marlborough cigarettes until she died of pneumonia a year later.

1988
THE FRENCH

Even though most complaints against the French are true—and given all of the bad experiences I've had in France—I nevertheless ignore it all and still appreciate *The French*, one of the great civilizations of human history.

In the following 1988 encounter taking place at my parent's house, please note that I arrive in good spirits to meet their French friends, yet get blindsided by one of the guests, though I retaliate quickly.

Background: my father's career spanned the globe, running the international division of Combustion Engineering, a company that made giant boilers for electric power plants. Besides having customers in many countries, Combustion Engineering also earned royalties and dividends by licensing its proprietary inventions to foreign partners, while also owning a minority interest in those foreign businesses. The largest such licensing arrangement was with Mitsubishi in Japan. But there were others, including a French company, where my father sat as a board member.

Upon my father's retirement, after working together for three decades with this French manufacturer, the French company wants to give him a thank-you gift: a few weeks stay in France at places like the *Hotel de Crilllon,* all expenses paid.

I get a call one evening in New York, a month after my wife Janna's death. I am 35-years old.

Le Hotel de Crillon, Paris

Father: *Hey, if you are not busy on Saturday, we are having dinner with the CEO of the French company I was part of. It might be interesting.*

Joe: *What's the occasion?*

Father: *They are giving us a trip as a going away present.*

Joe: *Why?*

Father: *They like me.*

Joe: *Really? That much? Ok, I'll be there.*

It is summer and my mother prepares an afternoon meal served out on the screened porch, a delightful setting. Travelling with the French CEO is a young manager, around 38 years old, both guys having the look and polish of the French upper crust.

At the time of my father's retirement, his company had just brought in a new CEO of their own, a guy from AT&T. This fellow knows nothing about electric power generation, and over the past months I hear a lot about the mismatch, my father glad to be getting out.

French CEO: *So tell me about the new CEO, what's his background?*

Some fluffy back and forth goes on for a few minutes, my father careful in his comments, and I finally blurt out.

Joe: *He's from the phone company. He has no credentials whatsoever for running an engineering concern. He will certainly screw up, operating as if still at AT&T, a monopoly that has no products.*

This kind of straight talk coming from me ends the conversation. But the French CEO gets what he came for; I could tell in how he looked at me.

Note: the AT&T guy proceeds to almost bankrupt Combustion Engineering, going on a corporate buying spree to assemble a conglomerate of companies that have no symbiotic relationship with each other. A few years in, and a crippled Combustion Engineering is sold to a Swiss company.

Then somehow, the conversation drifts onto World War II. I am careful in what to put forth as the French are a bit touchy on the matter. But I do not lead the dialogue, the younger

French guy does, and I can't understand where he is going, though an aggressive edge to his voice seems directed at me.

Maybe my bluntness about that CEO coming from AT&T has ticked him off, the Frenchman seeing me as young and arrogant, a crude American, something counter to his whole aristocratic standard.

For a few minutes this new discussion solely pertains to war events in Europe, but then, out of nowhere, he glares at me and blurts out:

French Guy: *Why did your government drop the second bomb?*

Silence at the table, and then I reply.

Joe: *Because after Hiroshima the Japanese didn't surrender, so a couple of days later we hit Nagasaki. Even then, it took them a week to give up!*

French Guy: *How do you know?*

Joe: *What do you mean "How do I know"?*

French Guy: *Perhaps your government lied to you.*

Joe: *Perhaps, but do you know what "Uncle" means?*

The French guy looks at his CEO puzzled.

French CEO: *We, oncle*, explaining in French that I literally meant Uncle.

Joe: *Well, in America, when two boys get into a fight and one gives up, he can't just give up. He has to say Uncle.*

French Guy, still not getting it: *Uncle?*

Joe: *It's just a word. Even if Japan surrendered after the first bomb, it wasn't enough. They had to say Uncle, so we leveled them again. You don't attack the United States of America and not say Uncle. Get it.*

Boy, what a screw up! These guys came all the way over from France to give my parents such a nice gift and look at my behavior. Finally, I catch the CEO's eye, and from what I can tell, he loves the whole thing: an attempt to box me in with *French sophistry* defeated by *American clarity*.

And besides *Vive La France*—and I mean it—that's all I've got to say about that.

A note on the Japanese surrender, follows. At the time of the above 1988 encounter, the end of World War II occurred just decades prior, still an anchor in one's mind. We still felt its shadow.

Note: *In what is called the* **Jewel Voice Broadcast**, *Japanese Emperor Hirohito accepts the unconditional surrender of the Japanese military. This speech was broadcast at noon Japan Standard Time on* **August 15, 1945**, *3 ½ months after the Battle of Okinawa on April 1st, days after the atomic bombings of Hiroshima on August 6th and Nagasaki on August 9th, and don't forget the Soviet invasion of Manchuria also on August 9th.*

The point: even after all of these defeats, including Okinawa, the Soviet actions in Manchuria, plus our atomic bombs, the Japanese waited until August 15, 1945 to surrender. Like most self-absorbed oppressors, the Japanese really needed to say "uncle" before relenting.

PS. Don't ever think of attacking America! We do "uncle".

1987
STEVE MARTIN (WITH JOEY RAMONE)

This essay is multi-faceted, so please be patient. It spans time and most of all, besides Steve Martin, it involves the late, great, Joey Ramone—my man! Sorry, you'll have to get through Joey to get to Steve.

Where to start? Oh I know, Joey Ramone. I assume that all readers appreciate the Ramones—BLIZKREIG POP, SHENNA IS A PUNK ROCKER, ROCKAWAY BEACH, PET SEMITARY—but just in case, here goes ...

Like myself, the Ramone "brothers" of the band "The Ramones", hailed from Queens, but not anywhere in Queens, they came out of Howard Beach next to JFK Airport. Back then, It was half Italian, half Jew, and a mob community. In other words, it was the worst place in America

A BABY BOOMER'S ENCOUNTERS

for W.A.S.P.'s, and hence the perfect petri dish to conjure American punk rock—something akin to the Blues Brothers portrayed by John Belushi and Dan Akroyd.

The Ramones—from America—surfaced concurrently with the Sex Pistols—out of England—two autonomous 1976 punk movements that surfaced in defiance of Arena Rock and Disco, go figure. I couldn't get enough of these aggressive bands. In the 70's, I easily abandoning my groovy blues rock musical roots for punk, writing punk, and getting punk gigs at CBGBs, Max's Kansas City and Hurrahs in Manhattan, plus clubs I have long forgot about in Boston. Below, Max's, the Glam Rock capital of the world

In the 1980's, my brother in law Jimmy, one of my band mates, moved into a slum apartment on Avenue C in lower Manhattan ... a Latino black hole neighborhood, the place Madonna frequented—apparently, and, of course, I would visit Jimmy on occasion.

Down in the A, B & C avenue zone, AKA "Alphabet City", sat a small "needle exchange" meeting ground called Thomson Square Park, a green place pretending to be natural. That's where I momentarily met Joey Ramone.

I am walking back from 6th street, where brother-in-law Jimmy "lived", up to the 8th street subway, and walk through Tomkins Square Park. Joey is there stumbling around, looking at the sidewalk for discarded marijuana roaches. Photo, Joey in action.

Joe P: *Joey, what's happening?*

Joey R: *Nothing man, just looking.*

Joe P: *Well, the area at the bottom of central park by those ponds is pretty ripe, if you don't mind the subway.*

Joey R: *Never been there. Thanks.*

Joe P: *See ya.*

Joey R: *See ya.*

And I never saw him again.

Fast forward to 1987. My partner Lucien and I have just signed a contract with my employer, European American Bank, to take possession of the Foreign Exchange Dealing System I had built for the bank. The agreement includes a service contract to maintain said system, so THIS IS F'n

AMAZING. (My Navy Officer father never voiced profanity, and so neither will I. The "F'n" is a proxy).

Well Lucien and I are in heaven flying up the FDR Drive on the east side of Manhattan in a radio car. Rather than yellow cabs, back then, one could sign up with a radio car service who would bill you monthly. This was way before UBER.

Not wanting to end the day, I propose dinner at Sant Ambrose on Madison and 77th, one of my favorites. The car heads for our destination.

On the car radio we hear the dispatcher pleading …

Need a car to pick up the Ramones.

Silence.

Come on guys, I need one of you for the Ramones.

Silence.

I ask the driver why such a problem.

The Ramones throw up in the cars.

Oh.

Lucien, my partner, a guy from Luxembourg, who witnessed the Battle of the Bulge at age 5, asks:

Who are these Ramones?

I am about to explain, but we pull up in front of the Sant Ambrose restaurant. I tell Lucien that I will tell the story once inside.

I had called the maître'd ahead, a friend of mine, so Lucien and I float through the restaurant escorted to our table. The place is packed. I am on such high adrenalin that on the way to the table, I continue telling Lucien the story of The Ramones and the CBGBs punk scene.

Like many Manhattan restaurants, Sant Ambrose—where I would also encounter Richard Gere and Claus von Bulow (plus others not mentioned in this book) has padded couch/benches all along the two main side walls, set behind a row of tables with chairs opposite.

Really a French setting, rather than Italian, if you ask me.

At the end of this cavalcade of intimate tables, at the far end of the line, sits Steve Martin and his wife, who, BTW, ate there often. Lucien and I are seated 18 inches from them at the next-to-last table in the long row.

I am on a tear describing the exotic punk band "Cramps" and describing how the "Steel Tips" lead singer opens his show by blowing himself up (using a bullet proof vest—I got to know him later), and then diving into the audience amidst all of the smoke. You see, the goal of punk is to put the audience in fear for its safety, a crime you might have heard of labeled ASSAULT.

Photo, that's Poison Ivy of the Cramps.

As my story telling progresses, Steve Martin and his wife slowly tilt towards us, coming much closer than the standard 18 inches allocated between tables. Steve, when on stage with his white suit, represents the very opposite of punk—i.e. sophisticated W.A.S.P. humor, and no one is better at it than Steve.

One of my favorite Steve Martin bits is "How to make a million dollars and not pay any taxes". He pauses and off handedly says "first make a million dollars". Something in his look and delivery always makes me laugh at this joke.

And don't forget, Steve is a pro musician as well.

Well finally, my story telling runs out of gas, and though Steve probably appreciated the momentary entertainment, I sense his competitiveness, and the possibility that he has had enough of me. In my silence, with Steve now just 8 inches away, I see him catch his wife's eye, begin to drift back away from me, and begin to formulate his own stream of consciousness, starting with:

The last time I was on the Letterman show ....

He sure showed me! I was cut down to size (sort of). And sure enough, that night at 11:30 there he was, with Letterman, two geniuses.

And that's all I've got to say about that.

1984
ED KOCH

Arriving for good in New York in 1979, I was lucky to have Ed Koch as mayor, though I hardly realized it at the time.

Looking back, I can safely say that Ed Koch was the most visible politician of my life time. Throughout his nine years as mayor I must have seen him on the streets twenty different times, thumbs up, asking everyone "how am I doin". And he looked right at you.

He once said that the only reason he goes to movies is to stand on line, so he can talk to people, politics his whole life.

New York was bankrupt. The Federal Government agreed to guarantee the city's bonds as long as the budget was balanced by a certain date. Back then, in 1979 when he took office and I had just located in the city, the place was grimy. Times Square, filled with drug dealers, pimps and peep shows was unbelievable, not that I noticed after my years in rock music. But other areas as well: Harlem a wasteland covered with graffiti, Union Square a place to get knifed, the Lower East Side a slum, the South Bronx literally smoldering and the Port Authority a kidnapping zone.

Like the city, these were my poor years too. On weekends I roamed the streets to kill time, getting my big meal at some point. With my wife in hospitals so much, I joined the Metropolitan Museum for $35 a year and sometimes went there both Saturday and Sunday, attending lectures and slowly acquiring a broad knowledge of the world's art.

So running into Ed Koch was normal. We were both always there.

The first time I voted in New York was in 1981, Me and 75% of the voters went for Koch. Three years later he won with 80%. This support answered his "how am I doin" question loud and clear.

One weekend at 5th avenue and 59th street, at the edge of the park, I see him coming towards me. His two thumbs are up, he looks at me and says "How am I doin".

Joe: *Mayor, for once why don't you ask how I'm doing?*

EK: *Ok. So how are you doin?*

Joe: *Great, and you?*

EK: *Terrific. Where do you live?*

Joe: *81st.*

EK: *Anything you want to tell me?*

Joe: *Well there's one thing.*

EK: *Ok.*

Joe: *You know those smoke stacks they put on the streets for the steam to escape?*

EK: Sure

Note: underground Manhattan has sewer, electric, water, phone, cable and steam conduits streaming beneath the streets. Steam heats many older buildings, rather than each building burning oil or coal.

Joe: *Well I've been on 81st Street for about five years now and the city never put one chimney on our block. Is that fair?*

EK: Turning to his aid, *Make a note, smoke stack on 81st.*

He gives me a fresh thumb's up and moves along, both of us chuckling.

Years later, with my four children from my second wife Laura, as we traveled through the city in cabs, I would point out the stacks, commenting: *Those lucky stiffs, why don't we get one.*

And that's all I've got to say about that.

1986
MIKE TYSON

Above, Trainer Cus d'Amoto and his adopted son Mike Tyson in 1985.

Joe: *Mike... to be honest, I'm scared of you at this very moment.*

Yes, that was my opening statement to the *undisputed* heavyweight champion of the world, and I meant it. The full encounter follows.

To begin, the American in me roots for the underdog, regardless of the underdog's accidents of birth. I trust that any American, properly motivated and trained, can figure out how to win. Personally, I lived by this creed, and so, in a big way, Mike Tyson, an American underdog if ever there was one, mattered a whole bunch to me.

"Undisputed" means that Mike won bouts against all comers in all three boxing leagues: The WBA, WBC and IBF, whatever these monograms stand for. All that matters is that he swept the slate, the youngest boxer to win a heavyweight title at 20 years old, winning his first 19 professional fights by knockout, 12 of them in the first round. One cannot imagine his ferocity and his uppercut.

Mike won for a while, but then lost big time, both in and out of the ring. Accused of rape, serving three years, squandering hundreds of $ millions, before reclaiming his heavyweight title again, later in life he ultimately redeemed himself as a person. So you get it. I pretty much rooted for Tyson while continually hating his outcomes.

Orphaned at age 16, taken in by boxing trainer Cus d'Amoto, I believe Mike born with a kind heart, forced by street life into his role as the baddest guy on earth. Like others in Brooklyn, as a boy, Mike raised pigeons, his first fight coming after a neighborhood kid tore the head off of one of his birds. The kids also go after Mike due to his "tweety bird" voice. To survive, Mike immerses himself into street life, becomes badder than anyone, arrested over thirty times by age 13.

Cus d'Amoto, the legendary boxing mentor, adopts Mike, trains and guides Mike to become world champion at age 20. A year later Cus dies and Mike stands alone again.

Word has it that with Cus d'Amoto gone, Mike has become unstable, dangerous and violent in his private life, as wife Robin Givens eventually tells the world on the Barbara Walter's show.

Then comes the rape conviction, Mike serving three years in prison. Re-entering boxing once out of prison, Mike fights Evander Holyfield twice for the title. This second coming of Mike's boxing career is where the shocking ear biting incident takes place. Mike bites both of Holyfield's ears before the referee stops the carnage in the third round. Once stopped, Mike goes on a further rampage against Holyfield's corner, even attacking the security team trying to control matters. I witnessed this twenty years ago on TV and I am still upset about it, though apparently Holyfield forgave Mike and they are close friends today.

But it is mainly Mike's devastating punching power that stays with you.

I recall one of his earlier, pre-rape bouts—scheduled when I was visiting Florida one year. We find a red neck "cracker" bar broadcasting the event, and I remember a sign in the bar's window, stating, *No Hats*. This is racial code signaling that blacks are banned from the establishment—though a handwritten sign concurrently proclaims: "Tyson Fight Tonight". That's all I remember from that night, other than Tyson's knock out of the challenger at 90 seconds into the first round. It was an upper cut of such force that it should have left the guy dead.

Ok, so having restored the reader's memory of Iron Mike, we can move on to the actual encounter itself which occurred in 1986, just after Cus d'Amoto's death, ten years before the biting incident.

As for myself in those mid-1980 days, if not going downtown to Little Italy or China Town for my Sunday meal, I simply walk over to 86th Street and Madison Avenue to the big Jewish deli restaurant. I order the same meal each time: matzo ball soup followed by a half-roasted chicken with mashed potatoes and vegetables, and two cans of black cherry soda.

There are two seating areas in this always packed restaurant, the two sections not in view of each other, with the door and cashier sitting in between.

I get up to pay my bill, standing on line in front of the cashier station when someone from the other sections joins the line. I turn, and it's Mike. At 5' 10' we are eye to eye.

He stares at me, no expression on his face. From this I rightly assume he might break me in two momentarily, but I manage to say:

Joe: *Hi Mike.*

Mike, in his tiny voice: *Hello.*

Joe: *Mike… to be honest, I'm scared of you at this very moment.*

Mike, his eyes relaxing in surprise: *Well I don't want you to be afraid of me. I just want to be on line like everyone else.*

Joe, now smiling: *Thanks champ. I'm a big fan. And I hope you have a nice Sunday like everyone else.*

I pay my bill and we nod good bye to each other—the big dramatic events of both our lives soon to come.

Years later I read that while retired in Arizona, Mike now has 300 pigeons, and I root for him some more.

Then comes Mike's 2014 cartoon series titled: *Mike Tyson Mysteries,* billed as "Mike Tyson, his adopted daughter, a friendly ghost, and an alcoholic pigeon solve mysteries."

In 2017, Mike launched a *Youtube* channel with Shots Studios, featuring parody music videos and comedy sketches. Looks like he's finally having the fun he missed out on growing up in Bed-stuy, Brooklyn. He has rediscovered the kind boy he once was.

Quite an achievement!

And that's all I've got to say about that.

1994
CLAUS VON BULOW

Living in New York City for thirty years can churn up all kinds of people. One of the most sensational murder trials of the era found Claus von Bulow the defendant in an attempted murder trial, his wife Sunny the victim, with the great one Alan Dershowitz his defense attorney. Right before Christmas in 1980, Sunny had overdosed, and stayed in a coma for 28 years before dying. Children from her first marriage accused Claus; the D.A. agreed.

Sunny in 1966

During my encounters with Claus, he lived at his girlfriend's apartment on 5th Avenue and 78th Street. You see, Claus carried Danish aristocratic blood in his veins and a degree from Cambridge University England, but not much money in the bank. His big marriage to Sunny in 1966, herself worth over $100 million, brought him to the highest levels of wealth, a mansion in Newport, a lifestyle we cannot imagine and a moral code different from ours. With Sunny in a coma, Claus teamed up with a new heiress, who came with a pad on 5th.

In court, Claus was convicted of murder.

Claus and Alan

Alan Dershowitz came into the picture at the appeal, after Claus was convicted. The appeal succeeded, claiming that Sunny died of prescription drugs, not insulin injected by Claus.

At first, my encounters with Claus were tangential, passing each other in the street, but as I earned more money we would find ourselves at similar restaurants, especially Sant Ambrose on Madison and 78th where we were both regulars.

I wanted no trouble, just dinner, but every time we ended up at Sant Ambrose together, he was always there first; I would enter following the maître d, and would suddenly feel his glare. I'd look at him, never in accusative manner, but he seemed to challenge me with a "wouldn't you like to know" demeanor. Sometimes I nodded, but nothing more.

As one walks up the grand inner staircase at the Metropolitan Museum of art on 5th Avenue (left), the names of major donors are etched out on the marble walls, Claus von Bulow's name among them.

Though I carried just my $35 membership card, for years I stood with the Met whole heartedly, knowing its every nook and cranny, even the curator's basement, which I had toured. One day I decided to re-visit one of the period rooms on the main floor, a giant two-fireplace dinning room with white marble fire mantles, a mahogany table able to seat 30, and many large oils.

Staring into one of the oils, letting my imagination go, a couple comes up to the same painting. I look up, Claus looks down at me and with distain in his Cambridge University voice, says:

Oh its you.

And that's all I've got to say about that.

1997
RICHARD GERE

My 1997 encounter with Richard Gere taught me something. Richard did not attain stardom by acting in blockbuster films. Richard acted in blockbuster films because he was Richard Gere, a natural born star.

In the summer of 1997, Laura, my second wife, and I had been married for six years, with two daughters, and a third daughter on the way. My company Wall Street Systems was doing great, and we were living the big life in New York during the Bill Clinton-era golden years.

At the time, I had recently joined Manhattan's Asia Society institution, to become immersed in all things Asian, including the plight of Tibet and its Dali Lama, in exile due to communist China's enslavement of the Tibetian peoples.

As it happened, one of Richard Gere's passions focused on promoting the Dali Lama here in America. The top monk from Tibet embodied two causes that Richard could dig: first, the wonton takeover of Tibet by the communist Chinese, and second the practical message of modern Buddhism.

On a hot summer Sunday in 1997, Richard's big Dali Lama event in northern central park called, and Laura loaded our two daughters, Codyann, age 4 ½ and Tara, age 2 ½ into our double stroller, and we worked our way past the park's reservoir to the stage area set up for the event.

Richard held the microphone explaining—to a crown of perhaps 2,000—all about China, Tibet and the core message of the Dali Lama. When the Dali Lama took the stage, he spoke slowly and clearly, giving the listener the chance to lean in. The message was simple, humans, no matter the circumstance of life, have the potential to craft happiness for themselves. Not that it can be achieved easily and often not achieved at all, but one should not shut down the possibility by saddling oneself with a belief that one's circumstances unconditionally define one's path.

He continued, and I lasted just ten more minutes. You see, upon hearing the Dali Lama's message first hand after having read his book, just bought at New York's Asia Society—the 95-degree temperature in the hot sun said that we could depart.

On to the main event. I phone Sant Ambroes, the Milan based restaurant on Madison and 78th Street already mentioned a few times in these encounters, and book a lunch table for the family.

Being a regular at Sant Ambroes feels great: the refined cuisine matches the restaurants refined service, a reflection of its capable and kind owners. Laura and I had our first date there nine years prior.

The maître 'd greets us warmly, giving us our regular back corner table so that the girls can float on the cushioned divan built against the wall facing out. Laura and I sit opposite the girls on chairs. The cushioned divan runs the length of the back wall with room for ten tables for two. Tables are combined as needed. The four of us have two tables together, and next to us a large group—in great spirits—sits with eight tables joined.

All of our neighbors over at the big table are middle aged, between 45 and 60, except for one striking woman of around 30 perched on the end nearest us. We order and finish our two courses, and I notice the big table still has not received any main dishes. Oh well.

But the big table suddenly comes alive, cooing and looking into the restaurant. I turn. It's Richard Gere making a fine entrance, nodding to his friends at the big table while smiling at those scattered elsewhere. Working his way over, he finally sits next to the stunning beauty, who he kisses. The older people at the big table are besides themselves exuding "oh Richard, you're so wonderful" waves of unending love from their pounding hearts.

Richard now sits just two feet from Codyann and Tara. Cody recognizes him from the park and asks me: *Why is the Dali Lama so special?*

Why don't you ask Richard? He knows the Dali Lama personally.

The two girls, dressed in identical Sunday dresses, get off the divan and stand between the tables—holding hands, facing Richard. Cody is about to do the talking when Richard visualizes what is about to happen. Quick as a cat, he lays down almost horizontally so his eye level meets theirs. The big table is besides itself in this Richard moment, and the whole restaurant turns to watch Cody say: *Richard, why is the Dali Lama so special?*

Girls you know that your mother and father love you.

The girls nod.

But they don't just love you a little. They love you as much as anyone can love anyone.

The girls stare into Richards eyes one foot away.

Well the Dali Lama loves even his enemies just as much as your parents love you. That's why he's so special.

The breath runs out of every person within range of this magical moment. Cody thanks Richard and she and Tara climb back onto the Divan, Richard turns to his entourage and the big table sheds tears of joy just being in his presence.

If a director had been filming, we would have heard the words "cut and that's a take"!

At this point, deep down I muse, *Wow, Richard might really be wonderful!*

And that's all I've got to say about that.

P.S. Ever since Richard's 1993 Oscar Award speech denouncing China, he has been subtly blackballed within Hollywood. The Chinese market is key to many executive producers underwriting films.

2004
ALAN KING

Many assume that America's post World War II cultural revolution was led by musicians like Elvis, the Beatles, and Jimi Hendrix. Even in the 1980's and 1990's singers like Bono and Willie Nelson jumped in with their Pro-Africa and Farm Aid type crusades to further this leadership illusion. But the real cultural transformation was spurred by ideas that came from the great comedians of the 1950's and 1960's. Dig it!

Everything about the comedian's art comes down to ideas, ideas about stuff, ideas about themselves, ideas that show things in a different light.

Some ideas are about day-to-day occurrences, simply revealed both clever and engaging. Other ideas deconstruct important things, like rigid social structures, taboo topics, hidden political agendas, tawdry government practices, fraudulent celebrities, unmentioned ethnic traits and so on.

Most comedians from the post WW II era had an edge in how they illuminated their ideas, some had more than an edge, and a few, held deep authentic rage in what they envisioned... all packaged as observations appearing within an organic stream of consciousness.

Even the mainstream Jack Benny's and Bob Hope's had a bit of the killer's look when delivering a joke. After all, jokes slay status quo dragons, and most comedians have dragons to slay and usually not nice dragons. To do so, they use words, their swords: biting wit and often angry humorous rants. Jackie Mason, Lenny Bruce, Joan Rivers, Dick Gregory and even Buddy Hacket come to mind, as does Alan King—our encounter subject.

My uncle Frank Delomo had been a life-long member of The Boys Club of Rome, a serious American-funded orphanage founded in 1945 to rescue Italian street urchins left by the war with nothing. Being a Rome institution, from the get go, many big shot Italian Americans got involved at the Frank Sinatra level, and the charity still ran strong in 2004 when uncle Frank called my Manhattan apartment from his home in San Francisco.

Frank: *Joe, did you read the materials I sent?*

I had read them. The charity's big spring gala bash was coming up and Frank and Dot (his wife and my actual relative) wanted us (Laura my wife and myself) to attend. Lots of biggies were slated to grace the grand ball room of the Waldorf Astoria on Park Avenue, the headliners: comedians Alan King and Robert Klein on the dais, and the Grand Marshall of the whole shindig: Billy Chrystal—three Jews entertaining 500 Italians—go figure.

Needless to say a fine time was had by all. Each comedian had ready material, but even to listen to them talk to each other and to the crowd showed how special they were, and how honed their "idea" craft stood after a lifetime of experience. Plus… Frank and Dot, who, over the years had left their "can do" imprint on me, shined as usual.

When departing, after thanking Frank and Dot and saying goodbye to the Religious and Hollywood dignitaries at their sponsor table, I called for a radio car to fetch Laura and I in front of the Waldorf. Walking out of the hotel onto Park Avenue I see Alan King and his wife also waiting for a car, us boys in tuxes, the gals in long gowns.

Joe: *Nice job tonight Alan, all you guys were terrific, plus everyone worked for free. Very moving.*

At this point in his career Alan did many, many charity events.

Alan cracking a joke: *I also worked for free when I started out but got good fast. My mother thought I was a disgrace.*

Joe: *You mean about your brothers being doctors, lawyers and Rabbi's.*

Alan, born in 1927, same year as my own NYC mother, was one of eight children coming out of a poor Brooklyn Jewish household with strong parents.

Alan: *Yea and I did vaudeville. Not so smart, but it worked out.*

Joe: *Alan you did better than that. You helped change America, you and the others, lampooning every rule we were saddled with. Even when I grew up in the 50's and 60's there were still three America's: English <u>WASP's</u>, Italian, Irish, Jewish and Polish <u>Immigrants</u> and <u>Blacks.</u>*

Today there's still class combat out there, but it's not sanctioned. Just ignore it and do your thing. Don't look back.

At this point I noticed Alan's wife tearing up, not really sure why.

Joe to Alan: *You were part of that change, you helped break the log jam, way before there was a Beatles or a Bob Dylan.*

Alan: *Thanks, no one ever put it that way, so thanks for that.*

Both of our cars pull up. We wave and depart. Later I learn that Alan at that time is slowly dying of lung cancer from all of his cigars. He dies two months later. No wonder she cried.

Alan describing marriage: *Ya know, when my father got married he was six foot one, he's five foot two now.*

From what I can tell, Alan was five foot two at marriage, and died six foot one, his wife at his side.

And that's all I've got to say about that.

1997
JANETTE CARTER

A long time ago in the 1920's a country man named A.P. Carter foraged the Allegheny Mountains of Virginia collecting hillbilly folk songs.

A.P., his wife Sara and her cousin Mabelle had a band — *The Carter Family* — and fueled by A.P.'s song collection *The Carter Family* repertoire became the foundation of American country music. My encounter involved Janette Carter, A.P.'s daughter, when in 1997 she invited me down to the Carter Family Fold, the family's music compound in southern Virginia. It was Janette that sorted out my attempt to become a true songwriter.

Now, ask yourself, like I did, why is songwriting so difficult and rare? At the time of my encounter with Janette, I wrote songs, but they were patched together without any underlying craft to guide me. As a wannabe songwriter, I was desperate, grasping at straws, not getting anywhere.

If you think about it, songwriting is the marriage of two phenomenal human faculties: music and language, each faculty an enormous domain in its own right. One is taught language and one is taught music, but one is not taught the merger of the two.

Songwriting, a combination faculty, calls for poetic storytelling infused within music. All along I figured that there must be a key to the whole song writing mystery, as others had mastered it. Wanting to understand this key led me to Janette, as follows.

In the mid-1990's I immersed myself into the parallel worlds of Black Slave and White Hillbilly folk music, the music coming out of rural America in the 1800's. The Hillbilly folk songs, called *Old Time Music*—not quite Country or Blue Grass Music—is the music A.P. Carter went around the mountains collecting. Learning about A.P. I also became familiar with his family, including the kids—the Carter Cousins—June Carter

Cash being the most famous cousin, after marrying Jonny Cash.

Photo, June and Johnny

In 1997, I heard that cousin Janette still ran the "Fold" at the old Carter homestead on Clinch Mountain Virginia and that music was still played there on Saturday's.

I can't actually remember why, but one Saturday in 1997 I find the motivation to—believe it or not—obtain the Carter phone number from the receptionist at the Martha Washington Hotel in Abingdon Virginia, the closest hotel I could locate in the Carter homestead at the foot of Clinch Mountain.

Sure enough the hotel receptionist knows all about the Carters and says: *They're still down there if you want to call on 'em. Here's the number.* I call and a woman named Janette Carter answers—a good sign.

Her voice gives away her advanced years. I immediately relate to her as I would my beloved grandmother, who passed 10 years prior. As we make our initial exchanges, Janette stops me and says I speak too fast.

Son we're not in a rush down here over nothing. Then, with a little mischief in her voice, she proceeds: *Now let me guess where you're from.*

Well I tell her that I hail from Connecticut (where I had lived for a while), figuring she will accept me more as a New Englander than as a born-and-bred big city New Yorker. Good thing we didn't have caller ID back then or she would've seen the New York area code.

So, at her urging, I slow my pace down and at some point we start to discuss music. Eventually I tell her of my limited ability to write only children's songs.

Trouble with grownup songs huh? She postures.

Janette tells me of her father A.P. that she knows songs *pretty well* and that I should come down with my family *'cause me and my brother Joe still have the Saturday night shows, 'specially in the good weather, but not on the porch like the old days, but inside the fold that Joe built, that's like a barn.*

She adds: *Don't need a reservation, just get your tickets when you get down here, and anyone who likes 'Old Time Music' is welcome to join in.*

That's when I ask: *What's 'Old Time Music'?*

Silence and then... *Son you better get down here soon, 'cause you ain't gonna be writin' those grownup songs like you wanna, 'cause, poor thing, you don't even know what a song is.*

Sounding tired, she says that she'd talk to me about Old Time Music when I come down to visit, and she hangs up.

Fired up, I get back on the phone and book a room at the Martha Washington in Abingdon. A few weeks later, my wife Laura, our two baby girls and I close in on the Carters.

We travel to Abingdon on a Friday. On Saturday afternoon we drive west from Abingdon through Gibson towards the Cumberland Gap, and eventually take a road north up towards Clinch Mountain and the Carter Homestead.

Once there. I rush the family to the old Carter store—a shack—so we can put our feet on the front porch where A.P.'s shows happened in the old days. The store, consisting of a couple of rooms, now comprises a museum filled with a lot of very moving "Carter stuff." After taking that in, we cross the yard and walk down to the Fold.

Photo, Janette as a young woman playing the auto-harp ... A.P.'s country store in the background

The Fold resembles a barn in its wooden construction and it certainly provides a barn feel, but Joe Carter—Janett's brother—built the Fold specifically as an indoor band performance space.

I guess that it could hold 500 people but latter Janette told me it seats 1,000.

Its foundation? A series of "folds" where each fold (or step) climbs higher on the hill than the previous fold. These increments cause the building to rise in elevation as you move away from the front, where I would soon discover, the stage stands, the audience benches looking down on the stage.

I walk in the door and a lady in her late seventies sits at a table talking to people arriving for the show. She handles the tickets. I wait my turn and ask: *Janette?*

She doesn't look up but recognizes my voice. *You must be the fella I spoke to from New York. Glad you could make it.* She raises her eyes with a look that says: *No more of that "I'm from Connecticut business" 'round here son.*

I smile a bit sheepishly as she tells me to *just watch the show for now*. She and Joe (her brother) will sing before the first band comes out and *We'll talk during the ice cream break 'cause I ain't singin' after that.*

Janette then takes a good look at my family and gives me a nod. We move off of the ticket line and sit down on one of the front benches with our backs to the audience.

Once seated, I notice a slab of concrete measuring, say, 20 by 20 foot in front of the stage, providing space between the stage and the benches. *Wonder what that's for* I muse. My toddler daughters go out and run on it until the show starts.

Joe and Janette walk on stage. Janette cradles an auto harp and Joe holds a guitar. They sit down and Janette explains what Old Time Music is and what it isn't. *Photo: Janette & Joe*

Despite just being told I still expect them to begin with some little country song. But instead they open with a song about wanting to die because life is too hard and has already gone on too long.

Another day, another night

And soon we'll be in heaven's light.

Dumbfounded, and given my Manhattan mentality, I wonder how anybody could possibly think it all right to sing such a morose song, especially with such plain, rough voices—and out in public no less. I felt sorry for them.

But after a couple more of these emotional outpourings, I start to understand Old Time Music fast.

Old time music does not concern itself with cosmetics. Rather, it portrays the most basic human experiences with as much plain talk and true emotion as one can muster.

Next on stage one of the local bands, if you consider West Virginia local, and the real locals get up onto the concrete slab to clog dance. *Oh now I get it.* I say to myself. Intermission arrives.

Janette sits back there by the ice cream station, which performs double duty, earlier as the ticket station, with people already lined up for their allotted refreshments. *Don't serve no liquor here,* Janette tells me, *we're dry,* and adds, *no cursin' neither.*

I ask Janette why she has a Bluegrass band rather than an Old Time band playing after her and Joe. *Not many Old Time ones left, so we bring in the Bluegrass folks as well, that's assuming they have a fiddle.*

She then complains about the young female singer in the Bluegrass band who, to me, possessed a beautiful voice. *She just uses lyrics as an excuse to listen to her voice,* Janette groused. *Should be the other way 'round. Use your voice only as much as the lyric wants.*

After talking about how her mother Sara and her aunt Maybelle didn't talk to each other for a long time, she shows me a CD of the two old first cousins when they reunited in the mid-60's *with the help of Johnny* (Cash that is). The two recorded 30-odd songs in one sitting before Sara (Janette's mother) *turned 'round and went back to her trailer in California.*

Janette handed me the CD. *Here start with this, and later on you can branch out.* We agreed to talk more after the end of the second set.

After the set finishes, everyone in the fold clears out, with only a few hangers on, plus the band packing up. Janette sits by herself at her table, which now sells memorabilia rather than tickets or ice cream. I walk over and she starts right up.

Now son, 'bout those children songs. Do you know why you <u>can</u> write 'em?

I reply that I didn't know.

It's because they're not 'bout you but about children in general. Your children songs are what bein' a child's like for everyone, so you're not embarrassed by what you say, 'cause its all general.

She pauses. I nod.

Now those grown up songs, you're tryin' to make 'em too much 'bout you, and that don't work. First there's not much to say 'bout yourself when it comes right down to it, and second, even if there is, you probably can't say it, 'cause it gets ya all embarrassed.

I stand with pursed lips like Rob Reiner in "Spinal Tap".

Ya gotta approach the grownup songs same as the children songs. What's happened to you happens to everyone. So let each person hear their story in your song.

She looks at me to see if I get it. I thank her, saying that I understood everything she's been telling me, not just then, but all evening. Then I paid for a few souvenirs (the cousin's CD was a gift from her), and I stood there again like an idiot waiting for more to come.

A.P., Sara, Janette
A.P.'s store near Hiltons, VA, ca. 1950

Ya all oughta be getting back to Abingdon. It's a long drive and the road's pretty dark. We say our good byes and as my family starts to walk out of the Fold she adds: *Remember what I told ya honey.*

And I never saw her again.

And that's all I've got to say about that.

1996
PRINCESS DIANA

In the hey days of running my software company Wall Street Systems, I commuted to Europe twice a month, often taking a night flight to my destination city, attending a meeting or a sales event, flying back to London that afternoon to catch the Concord back to New York. Phew! If staying a few days, my home away from home was *Cliveden House,* a palace hotel 20 minutes from Heathrow airport, across the Thames River from *Windsor Castle.* A Cliveden House regular for sure, all of the butlers knew me by name. Cliveden House below.

Arriving Cliveden at 7 AM from Heathrow one morning, my plan was to drop off my bag, take a shower and have my driver bring me to the Wall Street Systems office in London for a sales event I was to lead.

Cliveden Butler: *Mr. Patrina, welcome home. Do you plan to join us tonight for the ballet?*

Joe: *Ballet?*

He explains that a fund raising gala for the *National Ballet* is planned. The Cliveden Great Room to be converted into a theater, with a stage and lighting, and after the performance a formal dinner served, followed by port and cigars. *Below: Cliveden Great Room.*

I said: *Sure, I'll go.*

Butler: *Did you by chance bring your tux?*

I had not.

Butler: *Not to worry, we will arrange for one while you are in the city.*

My mission: one of the European Central Banks was coming to the company's London office, shopping for a system. A rival company had software features better catered to Central Bank requirements then our commercial banking offering, but I hoped to convince them that the slight differential in features could be made up, and that over the long term Wall Street Systems would be the better partner. After a four-hour session, the prospects left, and though I had shot a lot of well-aimed bullets, I felt (correctly) that they would stick with the other solution.

Driving back to Cliveden in deep thought about the loss, I forgot all about the ballet.

Pulling up to the parking area in front of the palace I see 40 or 50 Rolls Royce/Bentley type cars all lined up, drivers standing by, with aristocrats strolling on the lawn dressed in formal attire sipping Champaign. In the reception foyer, the butler hands me my tux and a pair of shoes, and I go to my room to quickly shower and change.

Once outside, a butler comes by and I grab a glass, and turn 'round to find myself face-to-face with Princess Diana. And I actually said:

Diana, what are you doing here?

Amused she responds: *What are you doing here?*

I explained that I flew in this morning for a London meeting, and was invited by the House to tonight's ballet. I introduce myself and ask if she follows ballet.

Actually yes; I sponsor the National Ballet

Oh, then the National Ballet is yours.

No, I don't own it. I sponsor it.

I know that, striking back against her sarcasm. *I meant your project.*

At this point she appears radiant, enjoying herself, and I sense she is laughing with me not at me. So I proffer:

I guess I am the only American here. Do you know many of the guests?

Know? Some are relatives!

Oh! Well then the ballet has the best sponsor possible, that's for sure. Look at these cars.

Quite a collection!

Right about then I realize that a whole lot of people with jewelry are staring me down, wanting their moment with Diana.

Can't wait to tell my daughters that I met a Princess, but some of your relatives here are giving me the eye to move on.

Don't worry about them. Enjoy the ballet.

We shake hands and I float away. I am in heaven, not just in meeting THE Princess, but because from what I surmise, we like each other!

And that's all I've got to say about that.

PS. The next year I returned for National Ballet night, this time with my wife Laura and our daughters Cody and Tara in tow. Another splendid evening for sure, but though still listed as sponsor Diana did not attend.

1999
ERIC CLAPTON

My encounter with Eric took place on the Concord, flying from Heathrow airport in the U.K. to New York's JFK. The incident proved an echo from his past.

From the get go, Clapton rose to guitar-hero super-star status. In the 60's someone spray-painted "Clapton is God" on a London wall, and the handle stuck. Later, as a challenge to Frank Sinatra, Eric also took the title "Chairman of the Board".

But it wasn't always peaches and cream. Eric's post-WW II childhood reeked with tragedy.

Raised by his working class grandparents, thinking them his parents, one day young Eric is told that his mom is really his grandma, and that Eric's real mommy is coming to see him. You see, Eric's real parents had abandoned him. They had scattered like the wind, neither one ever checking in.

The boy quickly adjusts to the "real mommy" revelation and waits in anticipation for the great day to come. The real mommy arrives and Eric watches her as she interacts with her own parents. Eric is immediately drawn to this younger woman, a real mommy.

At the diner table, Eric bides his time, finally breaking into the conversation, turning to his real mother, and asks "Can I call you mommy now?"

The answer: "No, that wouldn't be fair to your grandmother".

According to Clapton in his auto-biography, his very being shattered into a million pieces of pain and shame. This is the moment the artist was created. The moment where he no longer cared. After this, nothing gets in the way of self expression and determined selfishness. And so in his teens, Eric pursues his great ambition, and

no one ever gets near his heart again. Such a terrible trade off for fame.

And fame it was, great fame. After some teen years in poverty, he makes it into the Yardbirds at age 18, then John Mayall's blues band, and then Cream—Britain's answer to Jimi Hendrix. Everything he touches turns to gold.

But Eric stays wary. It's not just his mother, or some other woman who can hurt him, bands can double cross him too at the drop of a hat, so as his stardom rises, he easily abandons one band after another, knowing that everyone wants to work with him. And so he performs continually, with the likes of The Beatles, Delaney and Bonnie, Steve Winwood, Duane Allman, etc. …… and basically operates as a solo artist.

The flip side to wariness though, is extreme selfishness, with Eric getting anything he wants—namely girls and drugs. He is so determined not to be held back by rules that his recklessness will likely lead to his death. This is when his manager Robert Stigwood steps in to protect him, assigning a full time "handler" to shadow Clapton at all times.

My first Eric Clapton concert took place during this period, at the Yale Bowl, in New Haven in the early 70's. Eric wrote about this show in his book. I was 22, he 29.

The Yale Bowl is elliptical, and they set up the stage on one end, with about 40 feet of grass separating the stage from the stands. Us fans were told to stay in the stands, the grass area verboten, a kind of a moat separating the star from us riff raft.

To ensure this construct, 50 New Haven police stood against the wall to keep us in the stands.

Poor things!

At 22 years old, I fear nothing, and more, I despise authority. Plus, I am not alone. After a few songs about a hundred of us scale the wall and the cops back down. Now they stand ten feet from the wall. With our now victorious vanguard on the field, more youth patriots jump the wall, and the cops retreat again, and then again. Soon I am dead center, four feet from Eric, who is high on heroin (his words). I watch him taking in the scene. And for me, mission accomplished. Front row!

Nope, four feet was not good enough for some of the others, and they challenge the cops again, this time going too far. Suddenly ten or so punks are thrown to the ground, as others begin to rush to their aid. I am still four feet from Eric ducking bodies. Retreat not an option.

Right when it could really turn ugly, the band stops. Eric says he is done unless order is restored and he walks off. Some other guy takes the mic, to talk the crowd down, and then it

happens. It begins to rain. The punk fires quickly go out, and Eric returns and opens with … ta da … *Let It Rain*.

A good time was had by all.

Some forget that in 1991 Eric's four-year old son Conor

died, falling out of a 49th floor window. Considering Eric's horrible childhood, for him to lose this boy must have devastated Eric far more than his "Tears in Heaven" song reveals.

Through the years I saw Clapton many times, including during his actual peak moment at the Royal Albert Hall in London. Some call it "The Royal Eric Hall". The peak occurred with his first "History of the Blues" show, which he must have poured his whole being into to achieve what I witnessed.

Using vintage guitars from various eras throughout the 1900's, Eric progresses from turn of the century blues all the way up to modern times, showing us a staggering array of curator-like knowledge.

But more, every piece was played and sung to perfection, including Hendrix's "Stone Free".

This show—from start to finish—stands the most masterful performance I have ever seen by anyone.

Yet besides this good fortune, "Clapton" luck finds me another time.

After many decades, Eric puts Cream back together again, but for just six shows, three in London at the Royal Albert, and three in Madison Square Garden, New York. Word spreads that he does this for Ginger Baker, then in his 70's, and financially in trouble. Eric, Jack Bruce on bass, and Ginger on Drums will each clear $4 million. Above: Baker, Bruce and Clapton in '67.

My old bandmate Dave looks into getting us some sold out tickets, but they are going for numbers like $5,000 a piece on the secondary market, apparently bought up by all of those hedge fund guys in the tri-state area, us mortals squeezed out by the one percent.

But for the whole week right before the New York shows, Dave periodically checks the show's "sold out" website, and at 11 pm on Friday night, 200 hidden tickets are released at their $200 face value, and Dave grabs a bunch.

During the show, Jack Bruce's fret-board hand cramps up and he somehow gets through the song solely with his plucking hand. Eric does not play any of the actual Cream solos, and simply riffs, but the vocals ring flawless.

At the end they play *Toad*, featuring Ginger Baker; it's his African-styled drum masterpiece, which he performs exactly as he had back in 1968. This goes on for ten minutes, and at the finale, as Jack and Eric bow to the audience and walk off, Ginger sits at his drums, a wreck, exhausted.

His band mates return and lift him up, the three walking off together to the most thunderous roar I have ever heard. It proves the last Cream show. Jack Bruce dies shortly thereafter.

But what about the 1999 encounter on Concord?

Ok.

There he was with his low key demeanor sitting in the Concord Lounge like the rest of us. No one bothered him. We board, and Eric sits four seats in front of me. I soon forget he is there, as once Concord takes off one's main thought turns to God. Will God be merciful with me when this thing goes down?

Next, the stewardess announces "duty free", which always got to me, as the last thing the Concord crowd needs is duty free anything. But a hand goes up. It's Clapton. He's buying something. What could it be?

A minute later the stewardess returns with a carton of Marlborough cigarettes.

Again I forget he is there. But deplaning, we exit shoulder-to-shoulder and I ask: "Hey Eric, what's with the Marlborough's?"

He smiles and sheepishly admits: "It's a habit from when I was poor. I was always worried about my ciggies."

A great artist, but at heart, still that poor beaten up kid buying cigarettes on the cheap.

And that's all I've got to say about that.

Motherless Child
by Eric Clapton

*If I mistreat you girl,
I sure don't mean no harm.
If I mistreat you girl,
I sure don't mean no harm.
Well, I'm a motherless child;
I don't know right from wrong.*

*Please tell me pretty mama,
honey where'd you stay last night?
Please tell me pretty mama,
honey where'd you stay last night?
Well, you didn't come home
till the sun was shining bright.*

1998
AHMET ERTEGUN

My composition *Not the World's Greatest Generation*, starts: "*When I was born I thought life was long; every day we got a brand new song*".

The point, from the 50's to the 70's, I lived in baby boom heaven, the height, so far, of American civilization, the time when us boomers simply took the cavalcade of music for granted. We assumed music born to magic. Only upon recording my own musical compositions would I learn that this boon-of-hits came not through magic but through the endless efforts of a few stalwarts, one being *Ahmet Ertegun*, founder of *Atlantic Records*.

Two of my music recording heroes include record-mogul Ahmet and his "angelic" engineer *Tom Dowd*. Luckily, I had four brief encounters with Ahmet, the fourth, as you will see, delivering the real payoff. *Above: Ray Charles & Ahmet.*

Ahmet, of Turkish decent, founded Atlantic Records in the early 1950's, his breakout star: Ray Charles. At first, the label focused on artists like Charlie Mingus, John Coltrain, The Drifters, Aretha Franklin, Ray Charles, Wilson Pickett, Sam and Dave, and Otis Redding, but in 1967 Ahmet branched into rock, recording giants like Cream, Led Zepplin, Yes, and Crosby Stills and Nash, soon followed by Foreigner, AC/DC, Peter Gabriel and Phil Collins.

Tom Dowd, the genius, had studied music from childhood, but also possessed a vast aptitude as a physicist, participating while at Columbia in The Manhattan Project—an actual inventor of the atomic bomb.

After WWII, Tom joins Ahmet, using his clear vision of physical sound to pioneer

210   A BABY BOOMER'S ENCOUNTERS

things like multi-track recording. (above Dowd and Dusty Springfield, a sixties icon).

For those who know of what I next speak, it was Tom Dowd who, for Atlantic Records, recorded *The 1971 Allman Brothers Live at the Fillmore* double-album, perhaps the greatest live recording ever. (Allman's)

Each night, Dowd not only recorded the show the Allman's performed, but using a razor blade, spliced together segments of each night's tape to assemble the flawless guitar solos of Dickie Betts and Duane Allman that one hears on songs like *Whipping Post* and *Elizabeth Reed*. Yes, those solos are Tom Dowd composites!

So there sits the magic. Ok, now the encounter.

It starts with Ahmet and me being neighbors. For 30 years we both live on 81st Street in Manhattan, myself in an apartment, Ahmet across in a double town house from which his wife Mica runs a high-end decorating company. I see him occasionally but never approach him, until...

After establishing my software company *Wall Street Systems*, major clients in Europe require my taking two overseas trips a month. I fly over for one-hour meetings if that's what is called for. This is where *The Concorde,* the supersonic jet comes in.

OK, say I had a meeting in Spain…. Overnight I would fly from JFK direct to Madrid, check into a hotel at 8 am. My Spain team would wake me at noon, drive me to the client site for a 2 pm "make it matter" meeting, drive me to Madrid airport to catch the 5 pm to London—landing in London at 6pm (a one-hour time zone pick up)—where I caught the 7pm Concorde out of Heathrow, arriving in JFK three hours later, home for dinner, up bright and bushy the next morning, back in the New York office, gone for but a day. Are you following all of this? I did it dozens of times.

Well at London's Heathrow Airport, "Concorde" had its own lounge… better even then first class. For example, I met Henry Kissinger and Eric Clapton in the Concorde Lounge and never met anyone in Business or Coach.

So one evening I spot Ahmet waiting in the lounge.

Joe: *Hello Ahmet, my name is Joe Patrina, I'm your neighbor on 81st.*

Ahmet, with a gruff, mobster-like voice kind of whispers: *Yea, so what,* and turns away.

So I'm thinking *"What's with the 'so what'. I'm in freak'n Concorde. It's even better then First Class."* Oh well.

Months later I see him again at Heathrow and just wave hello. He gives me a cold stare.

One day at home I walk up 81st Street and notice a limo in front of his duplex. I peak into the open back door and see him fidgeting, all agitated, obviously waiting for Mica to come out, Mica taking her time.

Poking my head into the limo, big smile, I say: *Hey Ahmet it's me "SO WHAT". You know, your neighbor.*

He stares for a second and finally bursts out laughing.

Pleased that I finally got him I just say: *See you at the airport.* And I walk off. (above: his buddy Mick).

Some month's later he's back, getting a drink at the Concorde bar. I walk over, and hold out my hand to shake.

J.A. PATRINA

Joe: *Joe Patrina*

Ahmet: *Yea, from 81st. I guess we both take the bus a lot.* (below: with Zepplin's Jimmy Page).

After a bit of small talk, I broach this subject:

Joe: *I always wondered, over the years, which artist were you most impressed with?*

Ahmet ponders: *Good question actually! I've got to say Steve Stills* (of Crosby, Stills, Nash and Young). *When he came in everything was ready. Every song, every arrangement, all of the harmonies, every guitar part.*

Joe: *Wow!*

He played most of the tracts himself. You know Déjà vu? The way it sounds? Well he came in and it already sounded like that in his head. And he was always on budget. Yea he was the best.

What a scoop!!! (above: Stills in action).

And that's all I've got to say about that.

A BABY BOOMER'S ENCOUNTERS

1991
BILL CLINTON

My encounter with Bill occurred just two days after the Jennifer Flowers scandal broke. Boy was he in trouble (not).

Of course everyone thought he was in trouble except me and Bill. We read the tea leaves!

I'm a political junky; I follow everything. I had heard that Bill was a player back in the mid 80's when he made his mark as the very young governor of Arkansas. But it was his saxophone playing on the Arsenio Hall Show that opened my eyes early on. *This guy will be President some day!*

Then the process unfolded. Bill wins the Democrat Party nomination, next going up against George H.W. Bush, Bush an impeccable American patriot of immense proportions. H.W. was America's youngest Navy pilot in WWII, getting shot down twice. He started an oil company, became a congressman, became U.S. Ambassador to China, headed up the CIA, served as V.P. to Ronald Reagan, and then presided over the fall of the Berlin Wall, the Unification of Germany and the First Gulf War... and he lost to Bill.

It's not just that Bush lost while possessing all of these credentials, it's that he lost to Bill while Bill was mired in the worst personal scandal possible, which was the exact moment when our encounter transpired.

At the time, in 1991, my company *Wall Street Systems* was just three years old. Our office was in the New Your Stock Exchange office building on Broad Street. I had a corner office on the 32nd floor, and from there I could see past the exchange building to the statue of George Washington, which sat at the intersection of Broad and Wall. A wooden podium had been set up in front of the Washington statue for Bill to make a campaign speech, and he was scheduled to speak momentarily.

I step out of my office into the company's programming area and urge the employees to hurry down the elevator to catch the speech. The women tell me I am nuts to listen to the creep, and the guys claim they are going with Ross Perot (below).

Joe: *Are you kidding, this is the next president, you need to come downstairs now!*

Employees: *Forget it!*

Joe to the women: *You're all going to vote for him. Mark my words.* And I go to the elevators.

As I step onto the street I hear Bill's voice, but hardly, as the entire Wall Street community stands booing him, drowning Bill out. I push through the crowd to get close, and realize the speech has ended. Suddenly the Stock Exchange guys rush against me trying to get back to the exchange floor. I push on.

Suddenly I step into daylight, look up, and standing right in front of me is Bill. No one is with him, but thirty feet away, twenty or so people surround Hillary. Bill and I shake hands.

Joe: *Looks like you don't have many friends around here.*

Bill, chuckling: *Well, they still like Hillary.*

Joe: *I just want to say I am not voting for you, but want you to know you're gonna win anyway, no doubt.*

Bill: *Thanks. Where are you coming from?*

Taking Bill literally, I point towards my building: *See that window up there above the landing. That's my office.*

Bill: *A stock guy?*

Joe: *No. A software guy. I tried to get everyone in my office to come down but no one moved.*

Bill: *No one?*

Joe: *Don't worry. The girls can't relate to either Bush or Perot, so you will win them back, and the guys will stick to Perot, splitting the vote. You're in!* (above G Washington views the stock exchange flag)

Bill, looking over at Hillary: *That's the plan.*

Joe: *Well anyway Governor, keep a stiff upper lip, and no more screw ups!*

Bill shaking my hand again, closes by saying: *And I want to thank you for how much you're not supporting me.*

We both laugh and I wave goodbye.

And that's all I've got to say about that.

P.S. Perot went on to capture 18% of the vote, the largest take ever by a third party candidate. And yes, Bill continued to screw up.

Funny thing George H.W. and Bill became lifelong friends. Go figure. Maybe H.W. became the father Bill never had.

1999
LES PAUL

(Photo, Les at 93, in NYC)

What is the impact of the electric guitar on our civilization? When was the electric guitar invented? Who invented it? And what encounter did your humble essayist have with the inventor, one *Les Paul*? Details follow.

Luckily for me, Les—1915 to 2009—lived into his 90's in NYC allowing me to sit in his presence a few times, ultimately resulting in a great, cherished encounter. But first a few words about the second *Thomas Edison* of modern music.

Music, of course, was once acoustically made and heard without electronics: violins, trumpets, drums, etc. Actually, music stayed acoustic starting with the cave man evolving through Mozart and others until Thomas Edison invented the phonograph in 1877 and Les Paul invented the electric guitar in the 1940's. It is this gigantic sea change for making music that I refer to in writing of Les.

In 1940, Les started using record player needles to pick up the vibrations of his guitar strings, these sounds then amplified through his record player. At first, there were many physical issues stemming from guitar body vibrations and feedback, leading Les to experiment with the solid body electric guitars one sees today.

The problem was, that after inventing his marvelous guitar contraption, no one took him seriously for almost a decade, until Gibson Guitars finally stepped up around 1950.

But Les should not be understood in just this way. He was a great guitarist, as great as any, including the likes of Hendrix, Clapton, Van Halen and Knophler. Les started as a country cat, but morphed into jazz and blues, his fingers skipping across the strings like flat stones on a pond.

Then he meets singer Mary Ford. They marry and become huge 1950's stars selling many millions of records. Not only does Les play electric on these recordings, but the scientist in him incorporates other evolving breakthroughs, like sound on sound (overdubbing), so that his records feature four and five samples of Mary's voice in harmony.

Basically, Les establishes the technological template for modern music, a template extended further by giants like engineer Tom Dowd of Atlantic Records (discussed earlier).

His guitar, the *Les Paul*, would be made by *Gibson Guitars*, and bought by the likes of Eric Clapton (below), Jimmy Page and Peter

(Photo, me in 1973 with the blond wood Les Paul)

Frampton. I bought mine, a 1968 model, from a guy named Jose, in Hartford, Connecticut during the early 70's. Jose, the original owner, had removed all of the paint, and the guitar stood finished in a natural, blond wood manner. This guitar, which I still play today, is a work of art.

Ok, let's move towards the encounter.

(Photo: Duane Allman with his Les Paul)

It is a bit fuzzy as to exact years, but in the 1990's I would go to a particular jazz club in Manhattan called the *Iridium* to catch Les in action. He played there every Monday.

(Photo, Mike Bloomfield and his Les Paul)

Due to his arthritis and the injury to his picking arm—from a car accident in the 50's, where his elbow was permanently set in position to strum—Les liked to take it slow, but one could always experience the fluidity of his sound.

Whenever he asked for requests I would say "Swannee River", which he would play. Swannee River starts with a gentle pull of two strings that I like playing myself, so why not watch the master. From there it soars like a rocket.

After the show, most left, except for a few males who would hang out with Les for a while. Some brought their Les Paul guitars for Les to sign with the wood burning pen he kept at the club.

Once Les was with "his boys" a different Les surfaced, crusty, explicative and a bit rowdy with a lot of "f" bombs. We, his disciples, beamed, taking it all in. Looking at me Les would say:

Les: *Hey Swannee, how the f--- are you doing?*

(Photo, Jimmy Page with his Les Paul)

Sometime in 1999 I head over to the club and bring my blond Les Paul. Every Les Paul guitar has Les' signature implanted between the tuning keys at the top of the neck, as did mine, but most guys liked to get another signature from his wood carving set.

(Photo, Slash and his Les Paul)

At show's end, there are about seven of us hanging around. (Photo, Pete Townsend and his Les Paul)

Les: *Hey Swannee, what have you got there?*

I open the case and hand him the guitar. He looks it over, strums a few chords and grabs the wood burning unit. I freak.

Joe: *No Les, you'll ruin it!!!*

Les: *Then why the f--- did you bring it?*

Joe: *So you could play it.*

He puts down the wood burner, plays a bar of Swannee River and hands it back.

Les: *Here, it's baptized.* (Photo, Peter Frampton and his Les Paul)

And that's all I've got to say about that.

Swannee River

Way down upon the Swanee River, far, far away.
That's where my heart is yearning,
Home where the old folks stay.

RICKY MARTIN
2000 (PROXIMITY)

I write this episode for multiple reasons. First, I am a fan of Ricky and his massive hit "Living the Vida Loca". Second, I am a fan of Puerto Rico, having been there often, though it has perpetual issues. Third, I am a fan of 116TH Street in East Harlem ... I'll explain all of this in reverse order, starting with 116TH Street.

Once upon a time East Harlem, whose epicenter is E 116th, was Italian, now it is Latino. Weathering time, two powerful Italian Icons live on in that neighborhood: RAO'S and PATSY'S. I never got into RAO'S on 114th—except for a glass of wine—due to the movie stars who control it, guys like Di Nero, each having a personal table they allocate nightly to their cooing friends. But, thankfully, forever, both while I lived in Manhattan, and then every year thereafter once moving out to Connecticut in 2007, I ate at PATSY's on 117th, a mob and cop joint.

So for now, that's it for 116th, other than the fact that I love being on 116th for no good reason. Keep this vision close.

Next Puerto Rico. What can be said?

To start, while living in Manhattan, in those years before I had sufficient disposable income to enable me to leave the city, I actually looked forward to the Puerto Rican Day Parade, always held, somehow, on the hottest day of July. The parade starts somewhere downtown and inches its way up 5th avenue, squeezed in between a million PR's (Puerto Rican's), who, due to genetics, ignore the police barriers set up to keep people off the street and on the side walk. The other NYC parades all respect the barriers.

Instead, sheer human overload rhythmically pulsates with the flatbed trucks carrying half-naked girls and Latin bands. It lasts all day. In special years a massive thunderstorm hits and nothing stops, as thousands of PR's roast pigs in central park. The whole thing stands free, and as said, I had no disposable income at the time, so this was it.

In the late 90's I was finally making real money and began, also, to write actual songs. Ricky Martin, himself from San Juan Puerto Rico, had his big hit in 1999, and it and Ricky became some sort of "filthy, uncensored, gay energy" loved anyway by the prudish sides of society.

> *Upside inside out*
> *She's livin' la vida loca*
> *She'll push and pull you down*
> *Livin' la vida loca*

Look at this! Where are the prude censors when you really need them?

Anyway, I wrote a beautiful love song, with a Latin feel, that also had some Spanish in the lyrics. I felt Ricky—humanity personified—could kill it. But how to get it to him?

Because Ricky lived in Puerto Rico, and because I could now afford it, I booked a flight for my family of six into San Juan, renting a gigantic two-bedroom suite at *Il Convento*, the island's top hotel, set right in the heart of Old San Juan, and its blue cobble-stone streets.

I figured: Check out the island, and maybe track Ricky down, nothing to lose. Below the old Spanish lookout tower on the cliff in San Juan.

Below, the Arecibo radio antenna built into a sink hole in western PR.

I had set my song, *Bene Me Este Noche* on 116th street. A Latino boy comes to NYC for some reason, but now in the dead of a rainy night misses his girl. That's the whole song. Here are the lyrics:

Bene Me Este Noche
(Come to Me This Night)

Verse 1

Deep in the night in this lonely place
I'm here waiting for you.
Come to me now my darling
Before our time is through
I listen to the rain
And I call out your name
Oh can't you hear me calling you
And I won't let you down
No I won't let you down
Come to me and let me love you
En la norte

Verse 2

I look for a ray of the morning light
To be warmed by the sun
"Cause into the heaven's light
Our time will be undone
To look into your eyes
To hear your gentle sighs
Oh can't you feel me wanting you
And I won't let you go
No I wont let you go
Come to me and let me love you
En la norte

Bene me este noche
Back in my heart again
Bene me este noche
Back in my arms again

Bene me este noche
Back in my heart again
Bene me este noche
Back in my arms again

This is the real stuff! Ricky could kill it!

At *El Convento*, I chat up the concierge. He says Ricky's manager (a woman) is a regular at the upscale Italian restaurant just across the street. We go there that night: a five-star authentic Roman place in a 400-year-old building, oozing eternity. I chat up the captain, who points to a lone female sitting at a table. I walk over and hand her my business card:

Good evening, Senior Mendoza at Il Convento said I might find you here. Can you spare a minute?

Many minutes.

I am a song writer from New York, and out of nowhere I wrote this masterpiece—in both English and Spanish. I sang it a hundred times and suddenly realized it the perfect romantic piece for Ricky, and I want you to hear it.

Senor, you are so resourceful, tracking me down like this, and your family is precious, but I sit her in sorrow. Today, after all of our success, Ricky fired me, and has signed with an LA agent. He wants to get into movies. I am sorry. I can do nothing now.

Hence "proximity". And that's all I've got to say about that.

On 117th, with a legal coal-fired stove grand fathered in from the old days, sits Patsy's. You can't believe how good pizza is coming out of a coal oven.

2001
YOKO ONO

My favorite Yoko story describes how John Lennon discovered her. Friends of John suggest that he check out the work of an artist named Yoko Ono, on display at a London gallery. John attends, walks around looking at some far out wall pieces and then notices a ladder set up in the middle of the gallery. Something is pinned to the ceiling above the ladder. He climbs up and gets close enough to read. All it says is "Yes".

John is blown away by the purity of it and the rest is history.

He would later imbed the experience in the lyric 'yes is the answer", with his composition *Mind Games*. I would later offer the lyric back to Yoko during our encounter.

John, Yoko and their son Sean lived in *The Dakota* on West 72nd Street, a very special building, and I dwelled across the park in my studio apartment on East 81st Street, a very humble abode. Like many, I learned of John's murder from Howard Cosell during the Monday Night Football broadcast.

At the time of the shooting, which occurred at the entrance to The Dakota (left), a definitive interview with John spelling out the details of how John and Paul wrote the Beatle masterpieces had just been published by Playboy Magazine, and his revelations re-inspired my own ambitions to become a songwriter. When Howard (Cosell) proclaimed the shooting, I along with most everyone sat devastated, our imagination mentor dead.

Plus, with me and John both being Dragons (Chinese Zodiac) and Libras (Western Zodiac), I always believed we were certainly linked by some higher order, and now my cosmic older brother was gone.

Soon a great memorial event in Central Park is organized attended by tens of thousands. My sister Carol and brother Jim come down from Connecticut to attend along with my two-year old and one-year old nephew and niece. My sister Carol manages baby Laura, then one-year old. I am in charge of my nephew, Jimmy, who I call Mimmer, who is usually a delight, but after an hour crowded amongst a sea of mourners, he suddenly becomes a terrible two's baby. First he fidgets and then screams at having to endure the whole scene. When the moderator announces the count down to "the two minutes of silence" for John, I hold screaming Mimmer up in front of my face:

Joe, whisper shouting: *Jimmy listen to me. See all these people. They are all going to stop talking. Everything will be quiet. You have to stop crying or everyone will look at you.*

Moderator: *Two minutes of silence in 10, 9, 8, 7, 6, 5…*

Joe, rapidly: *This is it. This is it. Stop crying now.*

And he does.

John died in 1980. My encounter with Yoko happens 21 years later in the summer of 2001.

Because I had been overseas for two weeks, I want to take my own son Joseph, about to turn two on September 11, 2001 (yes), not to our regular coffee place across the street, but a few blocks further uptown to *Le Pain Quotidien* on Madison avenue. This Belgian coffee shop boasts the very best coffee, French-style breads and pastries. Once inside, though in Manhattan, with its wooden décor and long rustic communal tables, one experiences the Belgian countryside

Stepping in with Joseph, I place him in a baby seat towards the end of a long table, with myself second to the end. Around the table's corner an empty bench rests at the head of the table. We order and are served. Suddenly a woman sits down on the vacant bench, catty corner to me, Joseph between us. It is Yoko. My New Yorker mores kick in and I want Yoko to have her space, so I pretend not to recognize her. She orders and watches me care for Joseph.

Yoko: *He's such a well tempered boy!*

Joe: *Yes, and not just now. This is who he is.*

Yoko: *Do you bring him here often?*

Joe: *No. I've been travelling so this is a special outing. Are you a regular here?*

Yoko: *I live on the west side but stop by often. Their bread is my favorite.*

Joe: *Do you have children?*

Yoko: *Yes a boy named Sean, and he has a nice temperament too.*

Joe: *Then we are both lucky for our boys.*

After a bit more chatter, I pay the tab and get ready to leave. I contemplate that both of us lost spouses in the 1980's and that she never remarried.

Yoko: *Nice talking to you.*

Joe: *The same.*

I stand and pick Joseph up, and with a Dragon/Libra smile on my face I lean down and say:

Joe: *You know what the answer is?*

Yoko: *What?*

Joe: *"Yes!"*

Her eyes open wide and she chuckles at my whimsy, then she simply says:

Yoko: *Thank-you.*

P.S. Here are the lyrics:

> *Yes is the answer and you*
> *know that for sure*
> *Yes is surrender*
> *You got to let it,*
> *you gotta let it go*

2005
THE JAPANESE

My intimacy with Japan (Tokyo above) goes back to early childhood in the 1950's. At the time, my father worked in the International Division of Combustion Engineering (CE), a U.S. manufacturer of power plants. One of his customers was Mitsubishi Heavy Industry, to whom CE licensed patented technology, allowing Japan to build state-of-the-art power plants in Japan and elsewhere.

I did not realize, but this close relationship with Japan took place just a decade following the war. It showed the depth of thinking of America's greatest generation, especially the peace-time generals Marshall, McArthur and the great one Eisenhower, who weaved the devastated world back together again.

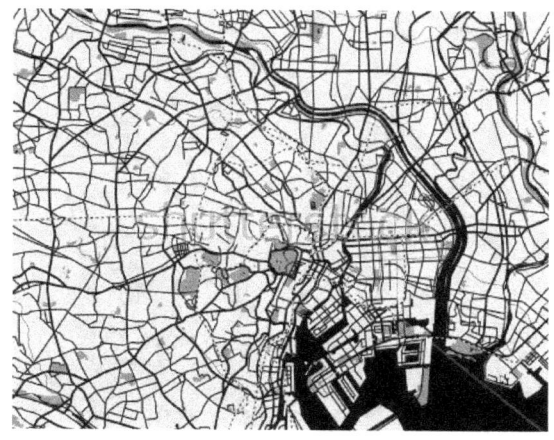

Left, Tokyo from the air

Well in my case, the manager appointed to work with CE by Mitsubishi became a regular at our tiny Long Island house. My father brought him home whenever the happy fellow travelled to New York for business. Us kids assumed him our uncle, jumping into his lap, thrilled to see him. Hence, the brilliance of both my mother and father in how they conducted relations with associates world-wide. Their combined career as American business ambassadors would evolve to legendary proportions.

Later, in my teens, other Japanese came through, with one family sending their kids to stay with us during the summer months.

Years later, my wife Laura's best friend turned out to be a charming woman named Hiroko, a Japanese national graduated from Harvard, working at SONY New York.

And so, "so far so good" for Japan and me.

But notice, this all took place in the New York metropolitan area. Up through this point in time, I had never dealt directly with the real Japanese on their turf, though this chance soon came my way.

Above, Emperor's Palace tower

In 2002, the largest Japanese bank, also the largest bank in the world, came into the market looking for a global foreign exchange system to tie their world-wide operation together. Since my company *Wall Street Systems* offered the only true-global trade processing platform, the bank came to see us in NYC. Left, Emperor's Palace tower.

Their scout was a young Japanese national who had graduated from Harvard Business School, while holding dual undergraduate degrees in both electronics and computer science. He spent many days with us peering into the ways and means of our technology and our service model.

Finally, he announced that Tokyo was ready to receive us, and that I must bring my top guys to Japan for a week-long exploration into our system. So off we go, me and my best guys out of New York and London.

My first observation: arriving at Tokyo airport, once in the taxi, other than my European/American staff, I would not see another Caucasian for the rest of the week. Everyone in Tokyo was Japanese.

Arriving at the bank, we walk across the skyscraper's empty three-story ground floor reception area to a tiny desk by the elevators. Three cute girls stand wearing pinkish-red outfits topped by Jackie Kennedy "pill" hats. They call upstairs and five managers come down to greet us. We will see no further females anywhere once in the business offices.

Our Harvard manager stays absent. Instead, this gang of five HQ guys are in charge. We set up our demonstration system in a room holding 50 folding chairs, and are told to start at 10 am by presenting our general ledger module for one hour.

At ten, 50 young Japanese men arrive and we present the general ledger module, not knowing who, if anyone in the room, speaks English.

Then we are told to present our counterparty risk module at 11:30. This segment-by-segment ordering goes on for days, often having us show the same module on different occasions to different groups.

Besides endless marching orders, day after day, we are never offered lunch, or even water, and we depart nightly without an evening invitation. We fend for ourselves in the big city. Luckily, my veteran team handles this quite nicely, though there was one hiccup on my part. You see, I found an Italian restaurant. We ordered pasta and it arrived covered with Campbell's tomato soup.

On Thursday night, to make up for the Italian disaster, I find a French restaurant in one of the big hotels and go for dinner with Hans, our six-foot-four German, who works for Wall Street Systems. Hans had initially met the Japanese Harvard guy back in New York, so this is his account.

Seated at the restaurant are numerous tables with a geisha girl and a rich older man. I had read that Thursday was geisha night. The men pay for all of the geisha's living expenses, but usually see their geisha only once weekly on Thursday nights. Apparently the housewives love getting these domineering husbands out of the house for an evening, so it is win-win all around.

I notice that no dialogue transpires between the happy couples, and Hans explains that the geisha's duty is to create tranquility for her sponsor, whereas the need to talk might cause pressure, and so, her sole purpose was to be there, beautiful, tranquil for him to gaze upon.

On Friday, we return to the bank.

We must have passed the test, as I am called out of the demonstration room, marched up to the top floor, and told to wait in an endless corporate staging area whose windows overlook the Emperor's vast, historical palace and garden complex sitting sixty stories below in the city center. I am brought into the office of the Global CFO, a charming man.

He has tea ready and sits me across from him on a long couch that can hold a dozen people. Two of his assistants are assigned to sit on either side of me, and he gets two assistants to sit either side of him on his giant couch.

I tell him that our short meeting is my chance to tell him the most important aspects of launching such a project, and that I wish to share perspectives gleaned through our 40 other bank projects. I ask him to please interrupt me at any time, but that I would otherwise present my points in short order. He invites me to begin.

Ten minutes later I make my final point, that over the course of a multi-year project, with so many personalities coming and going, things will occasionally go sideways, but that we should not over-react to each incident. However, if either one of us deciphers real turmoil we are to call the other directly. We shake hands; I am hired. From there, back in New York, my partner Lucien takes over, negotiating a contract worth many tens of millions.

The first milestone of the project is six-months out. It's a chip shot; just get one simple module installed to get things rolling.

Soon enough, I learn of a "wrinkle". Rather than installing the module "as is", the bank wants us to program a special sub-module that creates a report required by the Japanese Central bank.

To my guys, I suggest that we install the module "as is", according to plan, and temporarily feed their old system with data, letting it spit out the daily "2PM report" as it was called.

The bank managers say no, that they want to retire the old system completely, so we agree to digress a couple of months to build out this "must have" requirement—no big deal if this is the priority, though, of course, it pushes the "go live" date out—their decision.

Weeks after the original "go live" date passes, I get an urgent call from my Far East guys saying I am to fly over immediately. Heads are rolling due to the now reported schedule change. The top Information Technology (IT) brass has summoned me there in two day's time. The intellectual dishonesty in play is grating, but I book my flights.

Arriving Tokyo, like the Bill Murray—Tokyo hotel—character in the film "Lost in Translation", I do not sleep. At six a.m. I head for the pool, next meeting my Far East and On-site Project Manager for breakfast.

At the bank, we are escorted to a room with two long couches. Knowing the drill, I sit in the middle of one, and my guys flank me as eleven Japanese IT managers stream in sitting opposite me, the big boss directly across. He orders one of his guys to do something, and soon eight young Japanese desk clerks are brought in to fill out the remaining spots on my couch. Then it begins.

Big Boss has two pieces of paper, one in Japanese, and the other in English. He looks at point 1 in Japanese and then with angry, authoritarian voice reads—as best he can—the translation from the English sheet.

Big Boss:

Your company is NOT good.

Your management is NOT good

Your technology is NOT good

Your quawaty concro (quality control) is NOT good

Fourteen points overall. At least my mother has not been insulted! I sit stoically, thrilled at the whole "Bridge Over the River Kwai" spectacle.

The IT managers stare in anger; my desk clerks wish they were not in the room; my two guys sit in dread; I am to respond.

Joe—speaking through the translator:

Thank-you for inviting me here today, allowing us to learn from what has transpired.

Months ago at my meeting with the CFO—and warmly, I call him "Big Father"—we agreed to start the project with a simple goal, to gain a quick victory, and so I went back to New York with this as my focus.

To me, it was like "Big Father" had bought a new Toyota from me, and that I promised to deliver it on Saturday. I guess I am "Big Father" in my company, and I trusted my "son" to bring the new car over on the promised day.

But then the son of your "Big Father" talked with my son, saying that before bringing the Toyota over, he wanted to re-design the transmission. My son agreed to do this. They are both gifted engineers, so it seemed a good idea.

I heard about this, did not like it, but allowed it to happen, as the work was for your Central Bank.

And so, the delay is all my fault. You see, I promised "Big Father" that I would watch over what my son was up to and call if something appeared wrong. I never called.

I paused, and looked them all in the eye and finished:

But please admit, that you too are at fault. You did not watch over what your son was up to. And you never called.

When the translator finished with this clincher, every one of them snapped their heads down in shame.

Big Boss got up and walked out with the others saying nothing. I flew home on the next available flight. The invoices were paid.

And that's all I've got to say about that.

2003
ROD STEWART

Being a New Yorker, I often ran into Rod Stewart, another NYC resident. I guess we both needed to get out.

The first time in NYC—one glorious cool spring Saturday, sunshine dazzling—I am out strolling Madison Avenue along with the masses. About a block forward I notice pedestrians parting, like running water rounding a rock. What could it be?

Suddenly the rock appears forty feet in front of me, people scattering to make way. It is Rod with Britt Eckland, the former "Bond girl".

J.A. PATRINA

Nothing could be finer. Britt, a most beautiful specimen if ever there was one, on the arm of Rod, himself wearing a fur coat and proffering a hairdo obviously just blown out by his valet.

I now know the thrill felt by the peasantry as Nobles ride by.

(Jeff Beck)

In the mid sixties, Rod, the Scotsman, sings lead vocals in the *Jeff Beck Group*. Jeff is the guitarist of all times, and together they achieve perfection.

Their masterpiece: the spiritual *"People Get Ready"*. Dial it up!

In the late 1960's, British band shakeups happen. Steve Marriot (Ichigo Park) leaves *The Small Faces* to form *Humble Pie* with guitarist Peter Frampton (my favorite band of the era), and Rod joins the Small Faces.

By 1971, Rod has mastered his song writing, and Rod's new band—now simply called *"The Faces"*—releases a masterpiece album: *Every Picture Tells a Story*, which includes:"

Maggie May" and "Reason to Believe". They head out on tour (right).

At the Capitol Theater in Port Chester, New York, I sit, third row center.

Before the band performs, Rod appears with roadies in tow, wheeling out stacks and stacks of one-gallon wine jugs. These are passed out to the audience of, say, 2,000. As a jug comes by, no one sips; it is now or never to get one's fill. Soon, any buzz the audience came in with is significantly amplified. The band comes out and *Ron Wood* (who later joins *The Rolling Stones*) starts "Stay with Me" on his distorted six string.

Years later, Rod traverses through other musical formats, including disco, but remains an A-list star, living in Manhattan, playing soccer out in Queens, NY, but no longer with Britt.

Then, in the early 2000's, Rod and I often come face-to-face at our favorite restaurant "La Goulue" on Madison. This home to *swell people*—who are carefully seated day and night by James and Susan the maître d's—succors those unfortunate globalists enduring hardship, including Laura and myself, and as well as others, like Rod and Pierre Trudeau types (right, Melania Trump).

Back then, I am overseas every other week. When "at home", I try to end the week at 11:00 am Friday, with a NYC luncheon soon to follow. On Friday's I start taking project statuses and customer calls from Asia at 5 am, move to European calls around 7 am and finish the America's by 11:00. My ear literally burns from the phone! If no disasters surface, that would be it. Worthy news requires a call to my partner Lucien.

With this a reliable motus operandi, Jolene, my number three daughter, soon gets wind of the Friday lunch pattern, and while in the second grade she calls in sick on nineteen Fridays. I know this from her year-end, straight-A report card. Exactly as I hang up at 11 am on Friday's, she saunters down our penthouse duplex steps all dressed up, no longer dying of some grave illness. Laura and I shower and ready ourselves, and off we disappear into the city, often to *La Goulue*. La Goulue, by the way, was a famous French *Can Can* dancer in the 1800's.

On one Friday, we are the first at La Goulue. Laura and Jolene sit on the padded wall bench facing into the room's center, myself opposite them in a chair. There are mirrors above the wall bench; I can glance up and catch the goings by. BTW, it is Valentines Day, 2003.

I am a chatter box, thrilled to be there. Looking about I notice the place filling up, mainly with rich woman meeting for luncheons and a few businessmen as well.

I see both Laura and Jolene taking notice of something.

Laura: *Rod Stewart just came in.*

Joe: *Where?*

Laura: *Right behind you. He just sat down.*

I cannot quite see him in the mirrors.

Laura: *You sure got quiet. Are you plotting?*

Of course I was, but I needed a ploy. I notice that Jolene is drawing something with crayons on some paper brought with us. It's a Valentine Card. I look closer; it reads: **Dear Rod, happy valentine, from Jolene.**

You see, one of our favorite rock videos at home includes Rod performing "Some Guys Have All the Luck" in his red sneakers. All my girls learned to dance from this video, so Jolene, age six, means it.

I grab the Valentine, get Jolene off the bench, turn, and ten feet away sits Rod, perfect hair, a grey three-piece suit and tight tie, a gorgeous girl next to him, and an older lady also seated who appears to be part of his management team. All the women in the restaurant actually *coo* as Jolene and I step across. Truly we are on Manhattan's Upper East Side stage. Rod sees the piece of paper in my hand, gestures to me to bring a pen for him to sign his autograph.

Joe: *Rod, she does not ask for YOUR autograph, she brings hers, a Valentine Card.*

Rod: *Lovely, really!*

Joe: *Rod, it's amazing. Jolene must be the fourth generation of girls who knows who you are!*

Rod: *Apparently!*

Joe: *It's that video with the red sneakers, the kids love it!*

I give the paper to Jolene. She hands it Rod.

Rod: *Happy Valentine's Day Jolene.*

And he means it.

We all wave goodbye… like Frank Burns on "Mash" who once said *"It's nice to be nice to the nice"*. The whole restaurant coo's.

And that's all I've got to say about that, except that there is more Rod Stewart stuff, as follows:

Ten years later I take my family on a seventeen-day "total-immersion" trip to southern Italy. Initially, I receive criticism from my four children regarding the length of the trip, but they were totally off base… believe me!

Pursuing an amazing journey, enduring 115 F degree Sahara-desert overflow heat, travelling from the heel of Italy all the way to the Amalfi coast—with me driving—my family of six arrives at one of earth's joys: *The Palazzo Sasso*, in Ravello, Italy, on the Amalfi coast (above).

We are exhausted after the nine-hour heat marathon quest, and I tell Antonio, the *Palazzo Avino* manager, that we cannot have dinner at the hotel's 2-star Michelin restaurant as planned, but simply want a more informal meal at the equally gorgeous Palazzo Sasso cliff restaurant (Ravello is on a cliff, 1,000+ feet high, overlooking the Mediterranean Sea). Fine.

We go to our rooms. Shower and meet in the Palazzo's sumptuous air-conditioned bar room, which boasts an amazing collection of top-end drinks.

Bartender, knowing our situation: *Hope everyone is settling in after this hot day.*

He points through a bay window to the al fresco restaurant below: *That is your table of six if you change your minds, otherwise the cliff restaurant expects you whenever you are ready.*

I look out the bay window with the bar tender. Next to our empty table of six sits Rod Stewart and his new wife Penny Singleton (left).

Joe, to himself: *Oh well, it was not to be. We'll see him in the morning for breakfast.*

The next morning, I ask the tux-laden maître'd if Rod has come down yet.

Maitre'd: *Oh he just came for dinner last night.*

Joe, gulp: *Where is he staying?*

Maitre'd, pointing a thousand feet down to a gigantic ship anchored off the coast says: *That's his ship. He travels with his new bride.*

I am flabbergasted in how badly I miss-calculated reality. The ship was, I'll say it again, "gigantic".

Later that day, Manager Antonio arranges a 35-foot power boat for my family, which comes with a captain and first mate. We sail from Amalfi port to Capri (below), very proud of our boat. It was serious.

Arriving at Capri harbor I spy Rod's ship, and ask my captain to swing 'round it. We swing 'round, and on the back of Rod's ship hangs a utility boat bigger than mine. We are on a G—D--- minor safety raft!

Ok, to be complete, Rod's helicopter pad should be noted as well. And one more thing... *Some guys have all the luck!* Yea you Rod (you did good).

And finally, that's all I've got to say about that.

> *Some guys have all the luck*
> *Some guys have all the pain*
> *Some guys get all the breaks*
> *Some guys do nothing but complain*

2002
THE MOB

I feel compelled to convey my encounters with New York Mobsters. After all, growing up, the mob was part of America. *The Godfather*—considered one of the best films ever—told the story best, but *Goodfellas* did a nice job as well (above, real body bags at Spark's Steak House).

Rudi Giuliani's 1980's assault on the mob took place right in front of us in the New York daily's and on the Evening News. And though reportedly "taken down" by Rudy's vast prosecution of these thugs, somehow I still run into mobster's on numerous occasions in the 1990's and 2000's. I guess they survived! (Rudy the fearless, above)

Below notable mob encounters are remembered. Let's first start with John Gotti (below).

Scene 1: On a cold December day in 1985, mob boss *Paul Costellano*, on-trial, out on bail, and about to go to prison, goes to *Spark's Steak House* on East 46th for a "last supper" of sorts. Exiting his Lincoln Town Car in front of Spark's, Castillano is gunned down by confederates of *John Gotti*, Gotti a member of Costellano's own *Gambino* crime family!

In addition to all of the investigative and prosecutorial work done by Rudy and the DA's office, this assassination destroys the mob as we knew it ever since the early days of the 1900's. Gotti breaks the rules, acts alone, without the consent of other bosses from the famous five families: The Gambino, Genovese, Colombo, Luchese, and Bonanno families.

In desecrating mob code, Gotti makes enemies of the rest, allowing Giuliani and the Justice Department a way to pit one mobster against the other, creating a web of witness protection snitches that brings down the core of each family.

Just to give the reader an idea on Gotti, he goes after Costellano once Costellano says "no" to the peddling of heroin — which happens to be Gotti's main criminal business.

John Gotti — *the Dapper Don, the Teflon Don* — becomes larger than life in the Big Apple, seen everywhere, a celebrity taking in the good times, just as *time*, the families and the DA close in on him. Gotti's big quote: *I never lie because I don't fear anyone. You only lie when you're afraid.*

In the end, 1992, Gotti's own underboss, *Sammy "the Bull" Gravitano*, becomes the rat, his testimony putting Gotti and scores of other mobsters away for life.

Back then, amongst all of this drama, my favorite restaurateur was *Luigi Nanni*, a tiny 5' 4" powerhouse who had three Manhattan restaurants: *Nanni* on 46th (near Spark's), *Da Nanni* on 82nd across from my apartment on 81st, and *Il Valleto*, his masterpiece on 61st, where Gotti dined regularly.

Once a month I bring my well-dressed family to *Il Valletto* on 61st. We are a welcomed addition to this gorgeous three-tiered restaurant, itself clothed in Venetian wall coverings and upholstery. Always seated in the big dining room down past the smaller dinning rooms, my children are fawned upon— first by the hat check lady, then the captains and then, to some degree, by Nanni himself, though Nanni spends most of his time pacing and worrying that everything needs to be perfect.

The back corner table usually sits empty. It's Gotti's table, a perch where the Don can spy everyone coming down the stairs into the big, opulent dinning room. Apparently—according to the waiters—Gotti pays Nanni to fly live *Branzino* fish in from Italy to insure the freshest dinner possible. And with Nanni's wine cellar holding *Bogogno* wines going back to the 1940's, Gotti will leave with the waiters receiving a $2,000 tip on a $4,000 bill—all in cash—plus tipping the hat check lady $100 each night, even in August. BTW, she was quite gushy about the Dapper Don.

So when Gotti and friends are sent away in 1992, with the newspapers telling us the whole mob thing is over, I assume that's the last of it, hmm...

Scene 2: One day I invite *Yigal*, my customer at *Manufacture's Hanover Trust*, and my immediate soul mate, to an early dinner at *Da Nanni*, the Nanni outpost in my neighborhood. It's only around 5:00 pm when Yigal, my wife Laura and I step into

Nanni's townhouse restaurant. I say hello to the waiters who I know well and we are seated. But next to our table, a square table for ten stands waiting for a special party. We order.

Minutes later the entrance door opens and a huge guy looks in, turns and nods. A slew of expensive suits march in to take their spots around the special table, Nanni nervously greeting them, practically bowing to one of them. Immediately the goods are produced: wine, a wheel of Parmigano, hams, sopresetta, bruschetta's, etc., when some discussion transpires in Italian, with Nanni shaking his head "no". The big body guard is summoned, given an order, which he conveys to one of the drivers. Fifteen minutes later the guard brings in the huge jar of pickled things, which the table digs into.

In the mean-time, our pasta dishes arrive, and no one, least of all Nanni, will even look at us. We can't get grated cheese! The waiters each stand behind different sides of the mob table, removing any discarded plate, replacing silverware, pouring wine, as Nanni, in his chef sneakers, paces, sweat pouring down his face.

A kitchen boy brings out our main dishes, and takes the pasta plates. For a moment, Yigal, Laura and I sit quiet, just four feet away from the mob table, and then the head guy, a family head, no doubt, taps his glass, signaling the table with his hands to listen. He looks slowly around his table, makes eye contact with each of his "guests", and then speaks in a soft Mafia voice:

Friends are friends.

He pauses, looks around and whispers: *Friends are friends.*

Silence, and then it starts up again.

Passaic you're my friend. Passaic nods.

Newark, you're my friend. Newark nods.

After another minute of this Nanni looks at me. A waiter immediately bends down: *Forget the bill. Leave now.* And we do, the body guard letting us out, six limo's parked outside.

Scene 3: Years later, in 2002, my family of six heads down to my old haunt *Little Italy* for a Sunday meal at *Angelo's of Mulberry Street.* Angelo's does not take reservations, though sometimes, somehow—after arm twisting the maître d over the phone—when I arrive, the "Ronald Regan Table", which seats eight, is miraculously still available. My appreciation is, of course, appropriately shown. But this time being just six, we simply head down to accept any table available on such an important day—meaning Sunday on Mulberry.

The street is packed. Angelo's is packed, and we get seated in the way back, in a small room with seven tables, no one there. Like Gotti, I take the chair allowing me to look through the doorway into the restaurant, able to see its comings and goings. Soon a couple is seated behind us. We order, and after finishing a mind-bending antipasto course, I see the maître d leading four men our way.

They look dangerous, and that's because they are. One for sure is a "made man, Mafia Capo". He has sun glasses and wears his long coat like a cape, which the maître d carefully removes.

BTW, pretty sure this guy (left), Allie "Shades" Malangone of the Genovese family, was our Capo.

This Capo boss sits across with his back to me, his number two guy in position to monitor the restaurant. This number two guy is slender, but strong, like an Abe Lincoln, and I'm sure he has killed many. I keep turning to look at them, and the lieutenant always looks back.

They start with $300 bottles of Crystal Champaign, as a string of kitchen boys bring out the goodies. Every few minutes one of the restaurant's senior waiters comes by and kisses the Capo's ring. The wines begin to flow and they start singing Italian songs.

But then the language from their table, just a few feet away, gets pretty bad, the F bomb flying and my wife Laura becomes agitated that the kids are exposed. The slender watch dog seems to be watching us, whispering things to the Capo.

I hand my AMEX to a nervous waiter and tell him to ring up our bill pronto. While waiting for the bill, the slender guy walks over, and with an Italian accent he starts:

Such a-wonderful-a familia
Such beautiful-a bambinos

He takes out a wad of money and starts dishing out $20 bills to my four children, mindless of the money's value. I feel it prudent to re-assure him:

Thank-you, outside, we will buy something nice, maybe some ice cream or pastries. And thank your friends at the table too. (left Sunday on Mulberry)

With that he nods at me, making sure everything is ok, and goes back to his table.

I turn to my wife Laura, and say: *Take the kids outside. I will meet you once the bill is settled.*

Laura: *Jolene needs to go to the bathroom.*

Joe: *Ok, take her. Girls, take Joseph (age 3) and stand by the kitchen window until mom comes up with Jolene* (the bathrooms were down stairs). *Hold Joseph's hand at all times.*

As I wait alone for the bill, the slender guy gets up and goes out heading towards the bathroom stairs, but I cannot tell if he goes down or simply leaves the restaurant.

I quickly pay the bill. Step into the main restaurant and see the three kids looking at the chefs through the open window to the kitchen.

Joe: *Where's mom?*

Cody & Tara: *Down stairs.*

Joe: *Still? Don't move.*

I go down stairs, look around, push open the men's room, finding nothing, and then open the woman's room door.

Joe: *Laura?*

Amazingly, a woman says "yes", but I know it is not my Laura, so I race upstairs, grab the kids and go outside. Laura and Jolene are standing there on the pedestrian street. We must have gotten our wires crossed.

Yes, the kids had picked up a few hundred bucks, but we all knew that anything could have happened. A sphere of fear surrounds us, and it is not a good thing. That's what the mob does to you.

And that's all I've got to say about that.

2011—
THE HAMPTON'S (WITH THE CLINTONS)

My favorite August activities most certainly include dining at the Palm Restaurant in Easthampton, Long Island. Every Tom, Dick (and I mean *Dick*), and Harry from Manhattan is there battling for a table, and this bistro brawl keeps everyone from suffering pangs of homesickness for The City.

The Palm is food to die for, a great wine list, and Senor Romano, the fixture Maître d' who wholeheartedly keeps everything moving. Plus, they *always* have a lobster special for less than $100. But *Hamptons' Attitude* makes it tick.

We lodge 30 minutes away in Southampton, and so, harboring big plans for the wine list, I hire a limo to get my family to and from The Palm.

As we pull in, I tell my driver to wait in the restaurant parking lot. The valet says "No," informing us "*only valet-serviced cars can enter.*" I say I will pay for valet service and that my driver can play the part of wallpaper; we can pretend that I drove. The valet still insists, *"No. Sorry sir, I don't make the rules."*

Stepping into the restaurant foyer, I am greeted by the madding crowd, each guy fighting to secure the very table that he had already reserved. One fellow turns to me and cracks, "*Welcome to the worst economic downturn since the Great*

Depression." I muscle my way up to the reservation desk and check in.

A stylish young manager crosses my name off the main list and writes it down on a separate piece of paper—the "special" list. *"Table for six?"* he muses, suggesting that such a requirement dulls my chances of having dinner.

All around me, numerous testosterone-tinged millionaires hang about, looking—whenever they got a chance—at the "special" list. So when Senor Romano the Latin maitre 'd walks in from the dinning room to glance at the "special list", I make my move.

"Senor Romano," I insist, *"this"*, pointing to my name, *"is the most important guy on the list other than, say De Niro (who was on the list).*

But that's only IF De Niro shows up", I add.

Romano seriously studies my Latin-looking mustache while the dozen or so dining hopefuls press in around me and start to boil. Then after considering my Romano-like look, Romano says, "I will *work on it."*

And thanks to Romano's generosity in accepting the tip I gave him, we soon get our table. The place swirls and whirls with huge energy, as laser-focused, work-ethic-driven waiters run and gun all around us.

Yes, siree, we made it to the big leagues!

Our waiter, a Cuban hombre named "John", appears instantaneously. He presents me with the wine list, and then passes menus around. Quickly he returns with bar drinks; I place the wine order. He returns instantly with a Cakebread Chardonnay and a big time Cab. We begin placing our dinner order. It's go go go at every turn!

While decanting the red he suggests, *"If you want the surf and turf, then you should order whatever steak you want and then add the lobster special to the order.'* He points to the lobster special on the menu for just $98 and change.

"Fine," I agree. *"Good"* he confirms, *"I'll put it in the middle of the table."*

I go back out to find the men's room and some of the guys who previously had been in the lobby waiting with me WERE STILL THERE!

Trying to be funny, I point to the dining room and proclaim, *"It's a war zone in there, but it's worth it."* One chap chuckles, six other guys without tables give me glances filled with potential bodily harm -- mine.

Later on, during the dinner, my son looks around and asks, *"Are these 'FOB' people?"*

This question came about because Bill and Hillary were currently in the neighborhood enjoying the Hampton's. Their secret service contingent stayed at our hotel; I knew because we ate breakfast and joked with the agents each morning. I noticed how happy the agents all seemed. At some point earlier in the week I must have defined "FOB" as '"Friends of Bill" to my son.

Apparently weeks prior, Bill appeared in town with Joe "just kidding" Biden on a fund-raising campaign. During that trip, 25 secret service agents floated about, each one staying in a $500-per-night room, with a $200-per-day meal ticket, plus $1,000 per day in salary, plus $500 per day in benefits, plus $2,000 per day in long-term pension accruals, plus transport, plus gear, plus head office overhead—for a fundraiser! Who *wouldn't* be happy tapping into those kinds of government budgets?

Bill and Biden had finally left, but then a week later (my week) Bill returned with Hillary, staying at a $40-million-dollar mansion with friends in the Estate section of Southampton.

With Biden absent, and the Secretary of State here in his place, the Secret Service contingent numbered but 15. In the breakfast room, one agent commented that former N.Y. Governor Mario Cuomo had just been in town and didn't even enjoy the protection of a single state trooper.

I explained the difference by pointing out that we lived in *Winner-Take-All* America. Lady Gaga, who broke through to stardom, gets it all, and the 50 "would-be starlets" just below her -- who *want* to get it all -- get nothing. And so, Hillary Clinton, by hook or by crook, or worse ... made it to The One Percent and Mario did not, though Mario had a shot at the Presidency and fell short. I remember Mario on the convention platform looking like a mobster, lecturing "us the people".

All in all, I found being embedded in the Hamptons to be very exciting, especially with the Clinton's around. People were practically celebrating! Even the hotel people had had photos of themselves taken with, yes, Joe Biden. Limitless federal government spending was in the air, and the whole community was so proud to be supporting Obama.

I tell my son that after the Obama years of economic decline in America, that everyone, including Republicans, can probably be counted on as FOB's by now.

John, our waiter, informs me that after September 5th, The Hamptons will be dead.

"What happens to you?" I ask. *"There's a 'Palm' (restaurant) down in Florida. I get sent there. A lot of the customers here go there, too".*

"Go figure," I think, *"The party lives on".*

"And what about the hurricanes?" I inquire. *"You mean 'Irene,' the one that's coming here?"* he assumes. *"No, the ones down there"* I clarify.

"We're used to them there," he says confidently, *"don't make as big a deal about them".*

The check comes, we settle, and I call my driver. Standing outside as the car pulls up, the valet strides over and apologizes for not being able to secure my car in the lot.

"It didn't really matter to me," I point out, *"but now is when I would've given you the big tip. Ya see"*, I note, *"everyone could have gone home happy tonight."*

And we left.

Of course, at the time, unbeknownst to me or anyone else for that matter, this invasion of the Hamptons by the Clintons was just one move within their worldwide fund-raising *modus operandi*: Secretary Clinton sells influence, Bill and the Clinton Foundation get the money.

Natural born grifters! But one-per-centers none the less.

And that's all I've got to say about that.

2008
WALTER CRONKITE

Walt stands a titan off my youth. Not only was he the "most trusted man in America", the one who on CBS News told America that the USA would not win the Vietnam war, but before that, he was the "gung-ho on everything American" guy, the one who truly inspired everyone on a daily basis. His nightly sign-off: "And that's the way it is, February 5th 19…"

Many might not remember, but Walt was the great champion of American Industrialism, the host of the show "This Is Industry", and host also of the "You Are There" series, reenactments of the great historical events of the ages. Walt was the living voice of the Kennedy assassinations, the MLK demise, the anti-establishment and race riots, the burning of cities, the Space Program and everything American.

And so, I watched all of his stuff from early consciousness to around 1970 when I suddenly entered early adulthood and stopped watching everything but rock music for many years, strictly doing my own thing. I left Walt, and many other things behind. Like Abbie Hoffman, I went underground.

Years later, coming out of my fog, I watched Walt on TV again, finding him cynical, visibly down on America and a bit of a lefty. What happened? I'll never know, but my guess surmises his post-WWII, gung-ho heart broken by assassinations, the Vietnam War, Apollo 13 and Nixon, with only more crud to come as time marched on. Like all of us, he had lived in an American wonderland fantasy, and it all came home to roost.

Still, back in his prime, he was great. I hold great affection for him.

Decades pass, I am a "traveling idiot" for my company Wall Street Systems, flying overseas twice monthly, with domestic "day trips" interspersed. I run into Walt at La Guardia Airport in NYC. As it happened, I had just read an article describing how Lauren Bacall had recently sat on Walt's lap.

Now Lauren was one of my girls—like Marilyn and Jackie.

I had watched "Key Largo" her movie with Bogie a dozen times, more than the tally for Bogie's Casablanca. And though Lauren remained a New Yorker, I never encountered her ever! Geez!!!

And to think, she sat on this guy's lap.

So there in the flight waiting area sits Walter, in his wheel chair, with his wife, waiting right next to the gate for my flight, and I walk over with the big smile I naturally carried when out meeting the world.

Hey Walt, I'm not on your plane but wanted to say hello. Remember that "You Are There" episode about the British at Culloden Moor in Scotland, that was great!

Oh, you remember that?

Vividly.

You must have been quite young.

I just remember it. Plus, I watched the "This Is Industry" series too, great stuff.

Well thank you.

Bending down, whispering: *Walt, tell me if what I read is true. Did Lauren Bacall recently sit on your lap.*

Walt whispering, as his wife held his wheel chair: *Yes, but don't tell my wife.*

And that's the way it is November 5th, 2008. And that's all I've got to say about that!

2015
JOHNNY WINTER

It took a lifetime, but I finally got close to Johnny at Infinity Hall, Connecticut in 2015, a year before he died.

I have many guitar heroes, but none more so than Johnny, a true Texas gunslinger who played like lightning. He surfaces in the mid-1960s, signs with Columbia, and releases a few American blues albums that contrast sharply with the Eric Clapton, Jimmy Page and Peter Green types coming out of England. Johnny's voice, slide playing, straight riffing, look and movement on stage make him a giant of the trade.

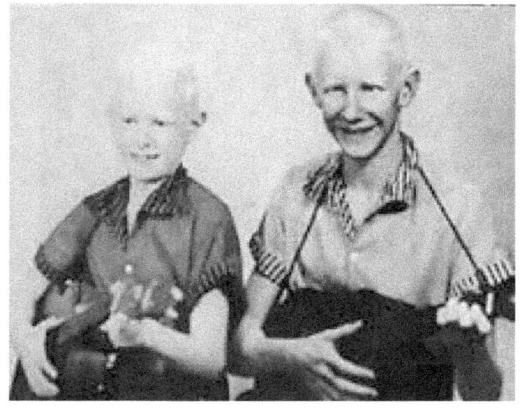

At the time of Johnny's rise, I am sixteen years old, and led to belief that Johnny, like his younger brother Edgar (right), are both soon to die due to being albinos.

Before this happens, I am desperate to see him perform and get my chance in 1970. Johnny has partnered with Rick Derringer (of Hang On Sloopy fame), having just released *Johnny Winter And*, with a gig booked (amongst others) at the Capitol Theater in Port Chester, New York.

My bandmates and I get tickets, but I am so freak'n stupid that I'm freaking out fearing Johnny will die before the show ever happens.

Driving south on interstate 91 from Hartford towards New York, with me at the wheel, our troupe is inhaling actual Panama Red. I go into a brain spin—visualizing that Johnny is about to die—then I realize it's me who's about to die and I start yelling, *"I'm going off the road"*. The guys quiet me down, I pull over. I am assured Johnny is not dead as another takes the wheel in my place.

The show overwhelms my idiot senses. Derringer (lower left) and Winter each have three twin reverb amps (this alone is heaven), Rick plays a Les Paul, Johnny his Firebird.

Finally, the finally: Jumping Jack Flash. I cannot contain myself and run down the center island only to be crushed by a stage hand. But I get to remain, though even to this day I remember nothing past that point.

Around 1999, after Studio 54 closes in New York, someone rents the space and over three weekends promotes Alvin Lee, Stevie Ray Vaughn and Johnny. My wife Laura and I, plus my childhood friend Sean and his wife Janet, attend all of these amazing shows, which come without seating, one stands five feet from the stage.

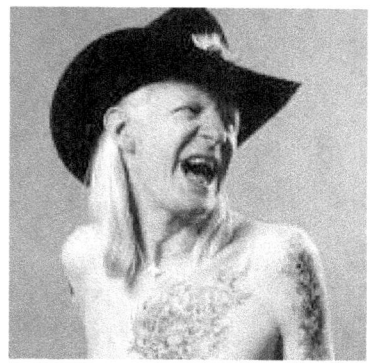

Johnny's bass player and drummer come out and go into the "boogie in G" pattern that Johnny always starts with to warm up. In the dark back stage, I see Johnny's white hair. There appears to be a ruckus. It's Johnny's road manager trying to shove Johnny out onto the stage.

Johnny resists, but a final shove has Johnny flying backwards onto the stage looking back at the manager.

Johnny turns, sees his audience. Johnnies sleeveless shirt reveals his tattooed body, covering up the heroin tracts. He is so skinny and frail that he plays a special guitar that has no body, just a neck attached to a board with pickups.

I am sick to my stomach, fearing the worse as I had decades ago, and then he hits his pickup switch, I hear a click, and suddenly he joins his rhythm section who has never stopped, and begins to wail in the most sublime manner imaginable. I am floored.

Right about then, a bunch of bikers, hugging the stage smoking cigarettes and weed, create a stir. One of them inadvertently burns Janet on the arm. When she recoils everyone notices. The bike gang forms a circle, assuming my friend Sean wants to fight the guy. In the mean time Johnny is deep into *Rocket 88*, a masterpiece. Over the roar of the band, we assure the gang not to worry. Let's watch the show.

Next: Johnny's version of Bob Dylan's "Highway 61 Revisited" soars.

Johnny finally goes into *It's My Own Fault Baby*, and we are all mesmerized by his output: then he walks off. Four songs, just like my encounter with Miles Davis. It must be the heroin.

So another 25 years goes by, and Johnny lives. I read his autobiography and cannot fathom how his survival is so. Massive, constant drug taking, causes him to fall down his stairs multiple times leaving him crippled. According to his book, his new manager, who also plays in Johnny's band, has taken over the job of caring for this thrill seeker.

I buy tickets to see Johnny at Infinity Hall in Connecticut, figuring this would be it, forever. They wheel Johnny out and he does his whole show sitting down, finishing with "Highway 61 Revisited". I next go to the bar for a nightcap, where I meet the guitar player/manager.

Joe: *You're taking care of Johnny now?*

Manager: *Yea, finally got him away from XXX, who is a drug pusher.*

Joe: *So how's it going?*

Manager: *A year ago he was taking twenty-two drugs; I've got him down to seven.*

Joe: *He's a national treasure, tell him I love him.*

Manager: *Hold on a minute.*

He goes to the bus out front, where Johnny apparently sits on a couch off his wheel chair.

A few moments later I get a pre-signed Johnny autograph.

Manager: *Johnny says 'thanks', he needs the love.*

A year goes by.

At B.B. King's Club on 42nd Street and Times Square, I learn that it's "come one come all" for Johnny's 70th birthday. I have to go. This could be it!

While there, I text my wife and *LittleHouse* bandmates up in Connecticut to convey the flow of the night. The place is packed with only us hardcore fans.

The following blog-like rant was well received, and so I decided to make it available here. Anything in parenthesis was added after the fact to explain things.

JOE—(LittleHouse Singer/Songwriter): *ALL: At BB King's for the big JW* (Johnny Winter) *bash. Show about to start. 5 guitar amps on stage, and many guests promised. Packed Sunday night house. We'll see.*

DOUG—(LittleHouse Drummer): *Cool, keep me noticed.*

TOM—(LittleHouse Guitarist): *My friend Allison Kaufman from Connecticut is also there! Petite lively blonde: say hello to her.*

JOE: *James Montgomery* (legendary blues harmonica player) *is MC, very pro, and chatty as ever.*

DOUG: *James always loved to yak and tell jokes, good MC. Sat in w him last year* (at a gig). *He invited us to Newport ...Johnny still sounding good?*

JOE: *Johnny just opened with "Johnny B Goode" and then launched into "School Girl", then "Mo Jo Work'n" with guest Papa Jo Chubby. Now it's a slow blues with some chick player: Holy Moly it's the Kaufman chick Tom knows !!!*

FRANK—(LittleHouse WEB Manager): *Their site says sold out.*

JOE: *Its SRO (standing room only), packed against the bar, and the crowd looks ugly: too many aging, dusty musicians in one place*

GARY—(LittleHouse Bassist): *Does that include you?*

JOE: *Of course not!*

BTW, the drummer is behind an arc of Plexiglas, just like Doug uses in the barn (the barn where LittleHouse performs in West Simsbury, Ct). *All guests use Fender amps, except for one Marshall. Also, guys missing hair—Johnny and the Bass player—wear hats.*

"Killing Floor" is up. LittleHouse dominates (LittleHouse plays "Killing Floor" too). *Waite on that ... Johnny is pouring it on. He's going for the finish line. Johnny's doing the original Electric Flag horn parts on guitar, the ones that Joe M badgers us to play.*

JOE M—(LittleHouse Producer): *Praise The Lord.*

JOE: *A young Texan with a cowboy hat is out. Pretty sure he has hair. A slow hand Billy Gibbons (of ZZ Top) type who can also fast pick like Johnny. Johnny and Billy are obviously this gunslinger's hero's. He uses that mentioned Marshall amp off to the side and plays a Les Paul* (Les Paul invented the electric guitar). *The Texan joins Johnny for "Summertime Blues".*

These guys actually have no material to speak of, crappy stuff that only works for blues/rock freaks—that's basically everyone here tonight, including me. Now it's" Jumping Jack Flash" with a quest guitarist playing a Flying V (a Guitar in the shape of a "V"). This guy plays in the pocket like Clapton, so I don't think he's from Texas.

Hmm... They're do'n a Delta Blues number. Hope it can go somewhere. The chick next to me already knows it is going somewhere. The lyric "Tell me mam a what the hell you gonna do".

Johnny is smooth. Now he takes off. Now he morphs into "Gimme Shelter". Phew!

A guy named Joel is introduced. What more Stones? Now they're doing "All Over Now". The chick next to me is beside herself and wants me to sing the choruses with her. Ok once "'Cause I used to love you, but it's all over now".

They just brought out Johnny's birthday cake and the chick is yelling at me for not getting up and shouting. How did this happen?

Next actual confetti is projected. Somebody, please kick those extraneous people off of the stage, including Johnny's wife, so that Johnny can play "Highway 61" (Bob Dylan's masterpiece re-interpreted by Johnny).

They're playing again. Ops it's "Statesboro Blues" instead of "61". Fine. A Firebird (a Guitar) *and a slide in Johnny's hands!*

Now she's pissed that I'm typing and she hits me.

LAURA (Joe's wife): —*Is she hitting on you?*

JOE: *No she's hitting me!*

Johnny's playing just like Duane (Allman); *it's a classic slow boil. Oh oh, a harmonica guest is drowning Johnny out. Give that guy the hook!*

Here it is ... the masterpiece of masterpieces, Johnny's version of "Highway 61". Johnny can do it in his sleep. It's so far out that I'm sure Texas Peyote (a cactus flower drug) was involved at some point (when Johnny arranged the tune in '68).

JEFF: (LittleHouse recording engineer)—*Niiiiice!!!!*

JOE: *It's over.*

Guess what folks ... It's 11 pm on Sunday night and Times Square is packed!

The chick Tom knows, Alison, I did not meet up with her but just chatted up James Montgomery and his girl outside the club on 42nd (Street). James still lives in Newport. Tonight some big player (a guy with serious money) in Greenwich is putting up all of the performers at his vast mansion.

I told James "You made it this far. Don't OD (overdose)." He nods. So does his girl.

JIM—(LittleHouse Multi-media): *He's playing around here in March.*

JOE: *Hold on I'll check ...*

James just said his band is playing at Bridge Street Live up in Collinsville, Connecticut on Saturday, March 22nd.

Check them out!

A few months later, Johnny really does die.

And that's all I've got to say about that (Photos, Joplin and Hendrix). He outlived them all!

2014
BILL COSBY

As I write this, Bill is 78 years old, blind, a shunned pariah in America, accused of drugging women who came to his hotel room for sex, so he could have sex without them participating in it.

This Quaalude drugging rumor about Bill circulates for years without prosecution, but it takes Bill's tirade against Obama—the 2013 *I'm Tired* publication where Cosby lists his grievances—to get the Department of Justice to take action. Within a month of the publication, the government has a whole bunch of women lining up to accuse him.

But, just as many overlook Bill Clinton's peccadilloes, or worse—due to Clinton's amazing talent—I want to say a few words about Cosby, also one of the great talents of my lifetime.

There are two Bill Cosby encounters, one in 1993 and one in 2014.

Minority groups live with natural fear of the majority. I experienced this myself in the 1960s as an Irish/Italian/German Catholic moving from New York up to Protestant Connecticut.

Minority rights is one of the reasons why the founders of America worked so hard on our Constitution and on our Bill of Rights.

But these formal protections do not shield one from every abuse experienced when growing up, especially in the kind of black ghetto Cosby came out of in Philadelphia during the 1940s and 50s. Endemic racial prejudice, poverty, absentee parents, a lack of high achievers to look up to... all weigh against a child in this environment. Yet Bill broke through.

Always the class clown and natural athlete, after his time in the Navy attending to wounded servicemen from Korea, and spending time at Temple University, Bill goes into stand up comedy, leveraging his stories from childhood, especially vaulting his main character *Fat Albert*. This gets him a TV role on *I Spy*, and from there he goes on to achieve lasting fame throughout his career, culminating in *The Cosby Show* his portrayal of black Americans capable of success—with no chips on their shoulders.

For decades Bill spoke up on the plight of blacks, chastising his people for having 74% of children born out of wed lock, the very antithesis of upward mobility.

Blacks being regular Americans is Bill's dream, and he rails against Democrats owning over 90% of the black vote, a pillar of the Democrat Party coalition of "victims". Hence his *I'm Tired* publication (excerpts follow), and the subsequent lynching of this "uppity Negro breaking ranks" by Loretta Lynch and Barack Obama.

I first met Bill in 1993 when we were both camped out at the *Plaza Wein Hotel* in Vienna, he filming the *I Spy* remake, and I installing *The Wall Street System*, my trading, risk management and back office system at Bank Austria. For weeks, at each day's end, we would both be hanging out in the hotel lobby with him smoking cigars and eying me across the room in his playful manner—making all kinds of cut up faces.

1968

1993

One Sunday my bank customer Armin comes to the hotel with his all-blonde family to meet up with my mostly blond family for breakfast, followed by an outing in the wine region on the Danube River. All the blondes go up to the buffet to fetch their vittles, myself staying put at the table, when Bill saunters over to me—the black haired one—and whispers:

They're taking over! A racial flip referencing blondes rather than blacks. Brilliant. Over the next days upon that foundation, we share a few more laughs and then the episode is over.

In 2014 my family is in Hartford having Sunday dinner with my eldest daughter Codyann, then attending Trinity College (as I had decades before), and at dinner I learn that Bill's one-man show plays that very night at the Bushnell Theater in Hartford, and that a matinee was just added for 5 pm. I want to go, but the family declines.

Joe: *Ok, just drop me off at the theater, and I will cab it home.*

At the ticket booth I ask for the best ticket and am offered something in row twenty (20) for $60.

Joe: *That's the very best?*

Clerk: *Well there is premium orchestra but they go for $84.*

Joe: *I'll take one. What's still open.*

Clerk: *Actually first row center is available.*

Bill comes out in sweat clothes with a UCONN Woman's Basketball, singing praises for this team that never seems to lose, ever, and then morphs into the shows theme: "women are in control" (hmmm…).

He sits on a simple wood chair right in front of me and keeps looking down, trying to figure where he knows me from. About halfway through he seems to have figured it out, as between bits he peaks down and makes some of the faces he used to make in Vienna.

Deep into the show, he pauses and asks me what time it is:

Joe: *As a guess, 6:15.*

A woman in the second row cuts in, holding her wrist in the air, showing everyone her watch, saying it is actually 6:20. As Bill's show theme is "women are in charge", he goes on a tirade in my defense saying my guess was pretty darn good and that this is further proof that women are in charge, always having the final word (hmmm…).

Bill to the lady: He said 6:15; can't you for once let something slide?

If I ever meet Bill again I will ask if he used this "what time is it" plant every night. I doubt I would bring up the Quaalude stuff. And that's all I've got to say about that.

A segment of "I'm tired" follows:

> I'm tired of being told how bad America is by leftwing millionaires like Michael Moore, George Soros and Hollywood entertainers who live in luxury because of the opportunities America offers. In thirty years, if they get their way, the United States will have the religious freedom and women's rights of Saudi Arabia, the economy of Zimbabwe, the freedom of the press of China, the crime and violence of Mexico, the tolerance for Gay people of Iran, and the freedom of speech of Venezuela. Won't multiculturalism be beautiful?
>
> I'm tired of being told that Islam is a "Religion of Peace," when every day I can read dozens of stories of Muslim men killing their sisters, wives and daughters for their family "honor;" of Muslims rioting over some slight offense; of Muslims murdering Christian and Jews because they aren't "believers;" of Muslims burning schools for girls; of Muslims stoning teenage rape victims to death for "adultery;" of Muslims mutilating the genitals of little girls; all in the name of Allah, because the Qur'an and Shari'a law tells them to.
>
> I believe "a man should be judged by the content of his character, not by the color of his skin." I'm tired of being told that "race doesn't matter" in the post-racial world of President Obama, when it's all that matters in affirmative action jobs, lower college admission and graduation standards for minorities (harming them the most), government contract set-asides, tolerance for the ghetto culture of violence and fatherless children that hurts minorities more than anyone, and in the appointment of US Senators from Illinois. I think it's very cool that we

have a black president and that a black child is doing her homework at the desk where Lincoln wrote the emancipation proclamation. I just wish the black president was Condi Rice, or someone who believes more in freedom and the individual and less in an all-knowing government.

Etc., for many more pages.

2012
JERRY ADAMS

In the fall of 2012, after returning from a family trip to the border counties of Ireland and Northern Ireland, my mother read an article in Connecticut's Hartford Courante about Jerry Adams coming to Quinnipiac University in Hamden, Connecticut.

Jerry, the modern face of the Irish independence from the English, was to inaugurate a new Irish museum that President Lahey of Quinnipiac University had built. The museum focused both on The 1800's Great Hunger tragedy and Irish art. Sensing karma, I felt the luck of the Irish coming my way.

I phoned my friend William Landers, who would eventually help me format my 2012 Ireland book. William had an Internet news site called *Ameriborn News*, and I wanted to see if he would cover the event. What is more, William had full reporter credentials, allowing access to people and events. Maybe we could meet Jerry.

Arriving at Quinnipiac, we lug his cameras into the gym; William presents his credentials, and we are told to set up in the isle on stage right.

We next speak to the school's PR manager, who introduces us to President John L. Lahey the school's president. President Lahey had led Quinnipiac for a few decades, elevating the school from college to university status.

We have a good talk.

I guess you can say that *Mr. Lahey* is all Irish, having been the grand marshal twice in New York's Saint Paddy's Day Parade but definitively, in his dedication in building the museum. *Mr. Lender,* who he points to sitting in a chair in the front row, is a major financial benefactor.

We ask about getting a post-speech interview with both President Lahey and Jerry. President Lahey says he can do it but that there is a lot of security surrounding Jerry's visit, and that the security agents will not allow Jerry to dally after the speech.

We all then get ready for Jerry to come out, with President Lahey stepping up to the podium to make the introduction.

The words Jerry spoke are in my Ireland book.

The speech was interrupted a few times by pro-IRA visitors who shouted out a protest or two against the English, and against the "soft" approach Jerry and *Sinn Fein* were pursuing with the whole English/Irish matter. They were removed by security.

After his address, Jerry stayed by the podium and greeted dignitaries. President Lahey came over to William and I for an interview.

As the interview proceeded, I kept looking back and kept seeing Jerry looking over at us. I could just tell that the politician in him was kicking in. *President John L Lahey* was on camera and the *President of Sinn Fein Jerry Adams* was not.

A few moments latter I heard approaching steps behind me. I turned. Jerry stood smiling at me.

As William got his camera ready, Jerry and I spoke.

I told him about the book I had just penned upon my return from the border area of Ireland, and said that his speech, of course, was very motivating, but that it also allowed me to benchmark what I had just written to what the living maker of history conveyed. I made a joke saying that my mother *Mary Lou Burke* (her maiden name), was worried about what I was writing, and upon hearing of my plan to attend the dedication said *"listen closely to Jerry and make sure you got things right"*.

For the record, none of what was written in the chapters of my book IRELAND, *Beyond the Pale* needed to be changed from what I heard from Jerry.

I also told Jerry that on the trip, my family went to the end of Donegal to see the abandoned village of crofter ruins— whose people had fled in starvation, boarding the "coffin ships" to America. This was a sacred place Jerry had visited many times.

William was then ready with his camera angle and he held out his microphone to start the interview.

Myself with Jerry

The interview first explored Jerry's connection to his 1990's sponsor, Bill Clinton, and then dug deeper into his dramatic life leading up to that time.

In the 1960's Jerry had come of age in a strict IRA family, with IRA members going back to the 1919 Irish revolution when Ireland finally broke free from England. Northern Ireland—where Jerry lived—stayed part of Great Britain. In the 1970's Jerry was gunned down by the British (machine gunned he said), and survived multiple episodes in hospitals, and served multiple sentences in prison.

And so it took to the 1980's for Jerry to decide to shun the direct confrontation methods of the IRA, and to instead pursue a political route towards peace, and eventually, towards north/south Irish unity (His political party *Sinn Fein's* ultimate goal).

Jerry got elected as a member of the British Parliament (representing his old neighborhood in Belfast), while also being elected a member of the Irish Parliament in Dublin. The long journey of using political levers, compromise, and incremental progress had begun.

Clinton, during the 1992 election campaign, met with Jerry and committed to the cause. Bill, part Irish himself, would help Jerry, and in doing so would win over many of the 50 million Irish American voters here in the states.

After the 1992 election, Bill kept his word—to the dismay of the British government—and got George Mitchell, the former Senator from Maine, and the ex-Senate Majority Leader, to be the USA's voice inside of the UK, to champion the Irish cause with Jerry.

And over time it all worked, as can be understood by that punctuating visit to Ireland by Queen Elizabeth almost 20 years after the political channel was pioneered.

(Elizabeth, left, dressed in Emerald, the only English monarch ever to pay respects to Ireland).

What a story.

And to think, this man, Jerry Adams, was standing in front of me, bullet hole scars and all; he was in his sixties now, still working the room and the cause.

Ay lads, Joe P speaking here … to be truthful, I be half Irish me-self! My "Galway" *Burke* family hailed from Queens, N.Y., and my "Cork" *Marshall* family came out of Hell's Kitchen on the west side (of Manhattan). My ancestors came to English America in those years when no one here wanted us!

And that's all I've got to say about that.

2014
GREGG ALLMAN

(Gregg, in 1971)

Today (2017) I learn that Gregg died. After all of my tangents with *The Allman Brother's Band* across five decades (1970 to 2017), I best remember Gregg through my final encounter with him in 2014, on a cold March night in New York City. We have a laugh, with Gregg turning out to be a real southern gentleman.

The thing about *The Allman Brothers Band* that I most admire is that Gregg kept the band alive ever since his brother Duane died in that 1971 motorcycle accident in their hometown of Macon, Georgia.

I witnessed the immediate fallout of Duane's 1971 demise on the band at an Allman's show in Springfield Massachusetts, a week after Duane's death. Miraculously, I got to stand on the stage and watch from the side as they poured their hearts out.

From that moment on, over the decades I follow Gregg, navigating many, many more obstacles to keep his band going. Indeed, Greg's perseverance teaches me to persevere with my own band endeavors. After all, once you stop it's over, and by "over", I mean that as the years' creep by, one will never perform in public again.

But to better describe Gregg's achievement, I want to clue the reader into one of the most insane human relationships ever assembled: *band dynamics*. You can't imagine what goes on!

I ought to know, as I lived in many, many bands. Say you are in a band and the drummer changes. That's a new band. Not sort of, but absolutely. Bands are specific personalities mixed within the cauldron at any moment of time. And for the band to survive, the immediate constellation of members needs to work.

Say it works. Great! But then certain members go through personal changes—new artistic designs, drugs, alcohol, breakups, suicide attempts, death! Or, subtler things, like when a bass player gets a commission to paint a mural, or a creative member feels the desire to go to Italy… this nonsense can cause a band breakup. I endured all of these. Inside of a band everyone involved can spiral out of orbit "in a New York minute"! Then the band doesn't work any more… just ask *The Beatles*.

And it doesn't matter how financially successful the band is or isn't, or how young or old the band members are. Once in a band you become "teenage imbecilic", oblivious to economic common sense or the boon of wisdom that normally comes with age. Paul McCartney suddenly hates Ringo's drumming, as Ringo is a great "beat" drummer, but does not adjust to straight rock. Plus, Yoko… "She's a bitch".

Look at *Crosby, Stills, Nash & Young*. For all of their talent, CSN&Y endured as a continual brawl. The band even fired *Steve Stills* at The Fillmore East in New York as they couldn't stand him for another minute. Drugs and debauchery playing a role. They took Stills back.

Of course to avoid all of that one can arrange not to be in a band. *Taylor Swift* is not in a band. Taylor Swift is the whole deal, with side musicians brought in to suit her current plan. At some point, *Eric Clapton* stopped being in bands, and now whenever out on tour, he takes new side people with him, leaving no doubt that this is not a band.

The Eagles found conflict when members, like Don Felder their guitarist, believed the Eagles a traditional band, Felder complaining that Glen Frey and Don Henley the singer/songwriters, make way too much money compared to the others. Things get so bad that Frey and Felder almost come to blows on stage, as seen in the documentary *The History of the Eagles*. Frey eventually fires Felder explaining that "song power" fuels the band's success, not some hippie commune vibe. The songs are owned by the writers, period.

The Grateful Dead, though, stayed a band no matter the differential of Jerry Garcia's greatness as compared to the others.

One famous case of not being a band is the *Stevie Ray Vaughn* saga with *David Bowie*. They should call him "David the slave driver". I remember Bowie's band rehearsing at *Complete Music* in the *meat packing district* of Manhattan.

At Complete Music, Bowie rents studio A and Studio B for three straight months before going out on that tour where he had that on-the-road heart attack you might have heard of. During Bowie's rehearsal stint, I'd rent studio C on some

Saturday nights, David's limo perpetually parked outside whenever I come by. His driver with a proper driver's "cap".

Arriving at 6 pm to jam with my nephews Jimmy and Scott, Bowie would be in studio A playing *Modern Love* over and over. When we leave at 9:30 for a meal at the nearby *Old Homestead Steakhouse*, they are still playing Modern Love. I say something to the guy at the front desk about how I hate the song.

Desk Guy: *They've been playing it since noon.*

Well on the Modern Love record, the guitarist is Stevie Rway Vaughn. On a tour that grossed over $100 million, following the release of Modern Love, David pays Stevie $750 a week, and won't give him a bonus. This slight causes Stevie to go out on his own and create great blues albums like *Texas Flood*. When Stevie goes on his own, he opts for a band thing, bringing in a bass and drum unit called Double Trouble: a great three-piece band.

Notably, over the years, Gregg Allman stuck to the band format, even when Allman bad luck got worse. A year after his brother Duane's death, Berry Oakley the bassist dies as well, once again, death by motorcycle. At that point, though, mercifully, Dickey Betts still carries on as ring leader behind the music.

It is Dickey who wrote most of the band's masterpieces like: *In Memory of Elizabeth Reed, Sweet Melissa, Blue Sky and Ramblin' Man.*

Gregg wrote *Whipping Post:* I'm still grateful to God and Gregg for this!

But band members morph. Old slights remain. New bad habits grow. Time grinds the memory of glory days and good times, and suddenly all of the joy of life is gone. And you never saw it coming.

If money is involved, as it was with The Allman Brother's Band, then these breakups are gut retching. The split between Gregg Allman and Dickey Betts is one such moment, a bad moment for us all. But the adolescent stuff going down at the time, plus the coke and the booze, make this fatal arrangement permanent (Dickey Betts, above).

Looking at my own past, seeing myself, remembering my most precious friends flowing through our bands, I can attest, that once push comes to shove, huge dramatic

eruptions simply occur. Participants of any age go after each other in rage, sometimes on the edge or past the edge of violence: reconciliations short lived at best. This is band life.

And so, I admire Gregg. And just think, while facing all of this band stuff, thankfully, Greg was married to Cher for a while! So now my humble final encounter with Gregg. It is charming!

As said, it was a cold March New York City night in 2014.

One of the city's top hotels is *The Surry*, on East 76th Street, between Madison and 5th Avenues. I love the place! So does the Allman crowd. It is a boutique hotel on a side street, beautifully appointed with a chic, happening, welcoming vibe. And in March one can snag a $850 room for as little as $450.

The next pawn on the board for this story is the fact that for years *The Allman Brother's Band* habitually played New York's *Beacon Theatre* every year in March. Over time, I think they played the Beacon a total of over 200 March nights. As a matter of fact, I saw the Allmans at the Beacon in 2013 with my friend Jerry, a year before the coming encounter.

So I am in New York in March of 2014 for no good reason at all (the best reason), staying at The Surry Hotel, oblivious of the fact that the Allman's are then at the Beacon, and further oblivious that they reside in my hotel. I am also oblivious to the announcement that the 2014 Beacon shows would be the last shows ever for the band.

My wife Laura and I prepare to go out for dinner, which means I am ready way before she is, so, as usual, I tell her to meet me downstairs in the lobby.

The lobby is pulsating with what are now called "the one percent", most of them liberals who somehow stand for the little people. I grab a drink from *The Pleiades* bar and sit in the lobby to take it all in.

A frantic guy with a ponytail sits down on the divan next to me and grabs the "house phone" which sits on the adjacent table. He dials a room. He is upset that someone in the room has not come down, and that others are already in the van outside, ready, though late, to get to The Beacon.

I add two plus two and calculate Allman Brothers. He hangs up.

Joe: *You're not having trouble with Gregg, are you?*

Road Manager: *No. Never Gregg. The band is at The Beacon, already past sound check. I'm trying to get the entourage together.*

Joe: *Who's the problem?*

Road Manager: *A couple of the wives. They're never on time!*

Joe: *Hmm... I know band life myself.*

Road Manager: *How so?*

Joe: *Been a player all my life. Now I write songs.*

Road Manager: *Really?*

Joe: *Yea. I had no idea you guys were here. Gregg is one of my favorite singers. There is one tune I have that I always thought might fit him, though it leans towards classic rock rather than blues.*

Road Manager, handing me his card: *Well send it to me. But only send me that one song. If you send a bunch Gregg wont listen.*

Shortly thereafter his entourage comes down and off they all go.

The next night I come down the elevator again in advance of Laura, having already forgotten the brief events of the prior evening. I pace the lobby waiting for Laura to materialize and I look through the hotel's entry doors out to East 76th Street.

It is March, quite cold, and hanging from the hotel's marquee are giant heating units radiating BTUs down on those hotel residents occasionally out waiting for a car. Two guys stand under the heat units. I continue to pace.

I look again and the two guys are still there. This time I look closer: two skinny guys with jeans and black leather jackets, one of them with a long grey ponytail. I have a *Damascus Road Experience* (look it up), and realize it's Gregg. I push through the revolving doors and like I've known them forever exclaim:

Joe: *Oh it's you guys!* They turn and laugh.

Gregg: *We thought you were our manager.*

Joe: *No I met him last night. He wants me to send him one of my songs.*

Gregg: *You're a writer?*

Joe: *Yea, and I have one called "Tonight Love Walked Out On Me" that you could kill, if you wanted a classic rock sound.*

Holding out my hand: *My name is Joe Patrina.*

Gregg, shaking hands: *We'll I'm pleased to meet you. I'm Greggory Allman.*

Joe: *Why are you guys standing here?*

Gregg: *Waiting for a cab.*

Joe: *On a side street? Where are you from, Georgia? Let's go to the corner.*

We go to the corner. It is their night off and they are going downtown for dinner someplace. We chat a minute more and I hail a cab. In they go, off into the night.

Greggory Allman, hmm… A very nice humble man, a band guy, and that's all I've got to say about that.

TONIGHT LOVE WALKED OUT ON ME

Tonight love walked out on me
For all the reasons that came to be
And now I'm left here with my life
Cut in two by loves cold knife

Tomorrow rain is gonna fly
Grey clouds come tumb'ling by
No need in call'n out your name
Life goes on just the same

But here in the morning light
I feel the firelight burning for me,
burning for me

2014
RICKY HENDERSON

In 2014 an Off Broadway play ran called *The Bronx Bombers* about the legendary 1978 incident where Reggie Jackson and Billy Martin "made contact" in the Yankee dugout (photo below).

Photo: Billy & Reggie having it out.

Yogi (Berra - left) and Thurman (Munson - right) needed to "fix things" before the boss George Steinbrenner stepped in. (George and Billy - center)

Luckily for me and everyone else there, Brandon *Steiner of Steiner Sports Memorabilia* hosted opening night. Brandon and a bunch of Yankee greats, including: Bobby Richardson, Bucky Dent, Joe Pepitone, Tino Martinez and Rickey Henderson, highlighted the pre-show cocktail bash.

After a few lively discussions with Brandon and the first four Yankee heroes, I eventually settled into a "technical" chat with Rickey – about batting.

At the time I was working with a few teenage boys, trying to convert them from hand-and-arm, little league swingers into classic MLB rotational hitters. Right there in the theater lobby I showed Rickey my hitting instruction program and explained the principles behind the form I advocate.

Rickey said I set up and rotated correctly, but based upon my explanation, he surmised that I did not truly understand the principle behind my correct swing. I knew the rules, but not the reason.

Yes, you set up well, and your hands and elbows move together near th*e body as you make the turn, he noted, but the reason you are squaring up correctly is that your stance makes you pivot through your core on your front shoulder, and the shoulder pivot then squares you up to the incoming ball.*

Huh? Then I stepped through what he described.

In all my years of swinging a bat, this key insight – how the stance and step cause the squaring up, power result – never occurred to me. Plus, I never realized I pivoted on the front shoulder and turned with my core, not my arms.

I had grown up merely copying the exact styles of my favorite hitters, which is probably why my swing mechanics are good, but I had never analyzed it very deeply. Above: Ted Williams – Crank, Step & Go.

Instead, as a kid, I assumed each MLB star's style different, but now Rickey made me realize that most of the great MLB hitters share a fundamental principle in kind. If one's stance is formed properly, then when stepping to strike the ball, one will use the stomach (core) to pivot on the front shoulder, allowing the back hip to swing around the front hip, like a gate on a fence post. Gates turn; they don't spin.

Suddenly I saw it. All of my young students were "spinners" rather than "batters". Instead of the front shoulder, their relaxed upper body stances caused the pivot post to run from their head down through the center of the body, between the legs and to the ground. This center axis stayed fixed, and the hands and arms just made a big circle around the centerline like a ballet dancer. Rather than pivot, they pirouetted – their core barely engaged.

And more, to stay stable during the pirouette, the young hitters barely took a step, if at all. As a result, they did not "bat" with their whole body; they "hit" with their hands, squashing bugs with their twisted feet and letting the bat fly away at the end of the spin, just to keep them from falling over.

After this, Rickey and I covered other ground in more detail, such as the **'stance'** stage, which locks the upper body in place so that it can only pivot around the front shoulder, the **"step"** stage, where one's load on the back leg and stride on the front leg builds the power supply needed to drive the ball, keeping the hands back as the core makes the first move, and the **"go"** stage where pent up energy is released in a squaring up manner,

perpendicular to the incoming ball – the whole body involved.

Funny thing, Rickey and I never discussed base stealing, though Rickey is the top guy of all times. Instead, he started to describe his conditioning regimen to my son, feeling we ought to value this first, considering his avoidance of injury across 28 years of professional baseball.

Crank, step and go ... the professionals really know how to boil it all down. Rickey is pure knowhow, and now he had passed a little on to me. *Thanks!* Below, Willy Mays all cranked up.

Then the bell rang and we were all asked to enter the theater for the show. BTW, the show was magnificent. Before the show: Henderson, Pepitone, Dent, Richardson and Martinez

And that's all I've got to say about that.

2015
ODELL BECHAM JR.

This more recent encounter shows that in 2015, despite my advancing age, somehow I still rooted for the future of America through one Odell Becham Jr.

In 2014 Odell came on the scene with the New York Football Giants (aka "Big Blue"), hailing out of Louisiana State University (LSU).

Louisiana—in case you know nothing about pro football—is home base for the Manning family, football royalty. Odell went to the same high school as had the Manning clan. Eli and Peyton threw to Odell in the off season, near New Orleans, where their father Archie Manning has his bar in the French Quarter.

Eventually, the Manning's got the Giants to recruit Odell, the ideal receiver for Eli. (above, adorable, aren't they?)

As Giants QB, Eli had already won two super bowl rings, interrupting the awesome New England Patriots during the Patriot's 10-year imperial reign, with Robert Kraft, owner, Bill Belichick, GM and Tom Brady, QB. The recruitment of Odell, therefor, meant much considering the stakes at the very top of the NFL food chain.

And Odell delivered—right away in 2014. Some of the most astounding NFL catches of all time came from the intersection of Eli Manning's passes and Odell's receptions. It seemed Odell's finger tips oozed glue able to stick to any football sailing across the universe. The whole world took notice. How could they not? In 2015 he had another great year, and expectations were high for 2016.

But hidden beneath stood a buried issue waiting to surface: immaturity.

Despite Odell's far out hair cut and the blond coloring scheme, no one really saw trouble coming, just some harmless immaturity leaking out all over the place.

I met Odell during the 2015 off season, right after his rookie year, 18 months before the embarrassing 2016 antics occurred, and two years before his Achilles heel injury came in 2017. In this encounter, none of my fatherly advice for him stuck. I did not affect his destiny. But I tried.

In March of 2015, when the encounter took place, Odell had reached 22 years of age, me 62. He was in Miami living it up. I too had gravitated to Miami with my wife Laura, our high-school daughter Jolene, and her friend Sophie.

We were at the Lowes Hotel on South Beach, each night hitting up one of my favorite restaurants. Next in rotation came Hakkasan, as good a Chinese restaurant as there is on earth, perched inside the Fontainebleau Hotel.

The Fontainebleau, a vast Miami complex operating since the the Frank Sinatra days, houses many top eateries and a night club. My father took the family there in 1966. Odell, of course, came for the Fontainebleau's *LIV* night club. But before getting to that, let's first have a word about Hakkasan. It is telling.

The first time I ate at Hakkasan I perused the wine list and found wines placed there by my friend Neil Rosenthal, a Manhattan wine merchant. This got me into a meaningful conversation with the Hakkasan sommelier (the wine buying guy). After some small talk, I asked: *What's with these wines going for two and three thousand dollars a bottle?*

Oh, don't you know? Hakkasan is owned by the Saudi Royal Family. They keep the wine cellars stocked at all the Hakkasan locations, New York, Miami, London, Dubai. If a regular customer wants one of these, then fine, they can purchase it, otherwise the

Royal Princes usually order them whenever they come through. Below; Hakkasan bar.

This fact, of course, made me feel thankful that the U.S.A. sent 500,000 American troops into Arabia during the First Gulf War. Lifestyles like these, need protection.

Well the meal was beyond belief, with me spending about $100 each on our white and red wine bottles. BTW, I tried not to feel like a failure when I ordered them from my new friend the sommelier.

Above: Fontainebleau complex

Next we are out in front of the hotel, on the steps, getting ready to fight for a taxi. I am preoccupied with the taxi challenge, until my daughter chimes in: *That's Odell Becham sitting over there.*

Where?

On the steps.

Sure enough there he was, in shorts with a knapsack, sitting alone, though surrounded by around 20 "brothers", his entourage.

Jolene: *Don't you dare go over and talk to him.*

Joe: *Why not, he looks friendly and I want to tell him something.*

Jolene: *Dad!*

I walk over, shake his hand and Odell gestures for me to sit with him.

Joe: *Wait'n for the club to open?*

Odell: *Yup.*

Joe: *Are you paying for all of these guys?*

Odell: *Yea, mainly.*

Joe: *This is not good. Odell, I know your rookie salary. The government takes half, and most of the other half is spent on your own stuff. If you keep doin' this, you wont save anything.*

Odell: *Yea, well...*

Joe: *Yea well..., say something happens, and you're left with nothing. You gotta rein it in.*

Odell: *Yea, I know.*

Joe: *Look, Odell, you're important in America right now. Everyone looks up to you, black and white. Somehow you made this Odell thing something above all that. You represent "can do", something America needs. Hate to lay all this on you, but being a role model is your destiny. You created it.*

Odell: *Yea, I can see that.*

Joe: *Ok, I'll leave you be. But remember what I said, and what's the main thing you gotta do?*

Odell: *Not get hurt.*

Joe: *Exactly. Have fun tonight, but cut these guys off. They're not in your corner.*

We shook hands, and that was that. Luckily Jolene took the snap shot posted here.

Unfortunately, after this, things went south for Odell—terrible on-field behavior and the injury—but hopefully, he ain't done yet.

Humans do not develop their "frontal lob" until age 26. That's the part of the brain dealing with judgment and consequences. Odell has time.

Looking back, Odell probably heard what I had said from his own parents, and was just being polite, hearing it again from another old guy.

But after watching him melt down a few times in the 2016 season, I wished I had offered to keep in touch with him, you know, to provide some kind of tough love. Who knows… he might have agreed.

In 2018, Odell's year-by-year option with the Giants expires. Anticipating a big contract, he was recently quoted saying he does not want to be football's highest paid receiver; he wants to be the highest paid player.

I still say: *Rein it in*, and hope he also strives for other important achievements, maybe being an American institution, like a Derek Jeter.

And that's all I've got to say about that.

Odell and I chat

2016
RUDY GIULIANI

Myself a New Yorker for decades, I find Rudy Giuliani a titan of the city. As district attorney, when he went after the mob, his small children threatened, I would wonder "where do they get guys like Giuliani? Without them, we would be slaves to the worst traits of mankind."

Then Rudy became mayor after David Dinkins, and straightened the city out all together, prosperity reined.

On September 11, 2001, as I tied my tie, my back to the window of my pent house apartment on 81st Street in Manhattan, my son Joseph comes in very animated. It is his second birthday and I assume he realizes this. "Let's go to the coffee shop" I tell him.

Down the elevator our doorman points to smoke that I never saw while upstairs, saying "a small plane hit World Trade." Crossing the street to the coffee shop, holding my son, we stare at the black smoke rising from the city itself.

Once inside I order our stuff and find a seat. Someone rushes in "The other tower was just hit." We all knew what that meant. Returning to the apartment the long, horrible death watch begins.

My wife Laura had taken our three girls to school and was having tea with the other mothers, not realizing what happened. I was frantic, wanting to get our Suburban up from the garage, load in the family and head north before another shoe dropped—one that never did.

By the time Laura came back it was too late, the avenues stood a sea of wall-to-wall people walking out of New York— in the hundreds of thousands! We head through the throngs to the school, get the girls and rather than sit in our apartment sit outside of my friend's restaurant, Quattro Gatti, having some food as humanity flows past.

When the human flood subsides at around 5 PM, I call for the Suburban, load the family, drive our baby sitter to Queens and head north, sure that the world as I knew it would never be the same, and it never was. The West has been in decline ever since.

But when the going gets tough the tough get going, and there was Rudy, with "W" and Governor Pataki, and the FDNY and the volunteers, and the rest is history.

Rudy was the first guy to back Trump, and he campaigned hard for The Donald.

Two weeks after the 2016 election I drive my family of six to NYC in yet another Suburban. We visit my in-laws Thanksgiving day and on Friday drive into mid-town to fetch my daughter at her job on 54th Street. On the way, I pull over at 52nd Street and run into Davidoff's of Geneva the Swiss Cigar company, to get a box of "Special R" cigars. Special R's use Connecticut shade tobacco leaves as the outside cigar wrapper, the leaves I picked as a boy on local Connecticut farms.

Coming through the Davidoff front door I spot him, Rudy, his back towards me, engaged in a lively discussion with the young jacket-and-tie salesman behind the counter. At the time, there is an expectation that Rudy is to become Secretary of State under Trump. Two suits with ear pieces stand guard out on Madison Avenue as the Mayor shops for cigars.

As I pass behind Rudy I squeeze his left shoulder, getting him to turn left, then squeeze his right, getting him to turn 'round the other way, where he gets his first look at my smiling, beaming face, and he smiles back.

Rudy, I want to thank-you for the election. You were the first guy in and every single effort proved essential.

Smiling, he shakes my hand and thanks me for saying so. Then I walk away towards the big walk-in humidifier as the Mayor picks up his discussion with the clerk.

Inside the humidor I take in the sights and smells of a few thousand cigars. As a boy, boys picked tobacco out in the fields and girls hung tobacco in huge heated barns. By late summer us kids would sneak into the tobacco-filled barns to startle our senses with a most amazing blast of cured tobacco scent. The Davidoff humidor was a hint of this.

I find my *Special R* boxes and grab one, hearing that someone else is now inside the humidor. I turn and it is Rudy and his clerk, looking at $40 dollar Davidoff's. I walk over holding my box.

Rudy, see what this is?

He looks at the box.

These are Special R's with Connecticut shade.

Oh yea, the best, do they still grow it up there?

It was called "Tobacco Valley" when I picked the fields in the sixties, but now hardly any is grown.

The clerk, proud to contribute: *They grow Connecticut seed in Nicaragua now, but still use the cheese cloth nets to create the shade.*

Hey Rudi, here is something worth knowing. In the late 40's Martin Luther King picked the same farms that I worked in the sixties.

Rudy: Never knew that.

Joe: *I read his letters to his mother back in Georgia, Martin was all wide-eyed about everyone in Connecticut. He said "there's no back of the bus stuff going on around here."*

Rudi: *I wonder if that helped to inspire his vision.*

Joe: *From what I read, undoubtedly.*

Rudi: *Very good to know. Enjoy the R's.*

Joe: *Well Mayor, you're the best and I hope things work out.*

I left and he went back to buying cigars. He did not get Secretary of State, but was put in charge of Cyber Security. I hope he figures out what to do. I sure can't.

TOM BROKAW
1979 TO 2007

Tom, my neighbor for 36 years, and I never got a hello. How could this be? Finally, in 2007, right when I was moving out of New York headed for Connecticut, a brief, telling encounter transpired.

Dan Rather – CBS

In the 80', 90's and 2000's, along with Peter Jennings and Dan Rather, Tom was one of the faces of the big three networks.

Peter Jennings – ABC

Brokaw — NBC

Tom, born in 1940, twelve years my senior, came out of North Dakota, and he sure made his way in life, becoming NBC's managing editor of the nightly news from 1982 to 2004. Plus, he wrote the book "The Greatest Generation" about our parent's generation, the ones who made it through the depression, WW II and the Cold War, re-building America, making it great again.

This was back before cable news, which as we experienced, turned the news into propaganda.

Still, it seems that ever since Walter Cronkite told America we were losing the Vietnam War, that all subsequent newscasters felt that they too could be a Cronkite and be the news, or at least be the enlightened leaders of us ragged masses. By assuming this role, in their own minds at least, they certainly deserve status as a special version of the 1%, living rich, famous and important.

Above, Park Avenue

So what's my beef with Tom?

Like I said, he never said hello. Ever!

Our Manhattan apartments sat across from each other at the intersection of Park Avenue and 81st Street. He had a five-bedroom sprawl, me a studio with a pull-down murphy bed. Left: Park Avenue

But as far as I was concerned we were neighbors, with both of us American adventurers representing the next generation.

We bumped into each other on many nights, he walking his dog on the corner, me smoking a cigar. I would often nod, but he looked right through me.

My mother said that he was a very nice man. She met Tom on a Quantas Airline flight to Australia. The Brokaw's were sitting in first class with my parents for 15 hours, so they had plenty of time to get a few pleasantries in with each other. The four Brokaw children were flying further back in the plane, but kept popping in to see their parents. Charming, or as Frank Burns of M.A.S.H. would say: "It's nice to be nice to the nice."

I remember when his book "The Greatest Generation" came out. I agreed with its assertion, but felt slighted that I, for one, and many of my baby boomers, were simply running a different kind of gauntlet than had our parent's. We nevertheless ran hard, demonstrated a great work ethic and certainly did not lack in American imagination. I wanted to say something about this to Tom, but my attempt fizzled out.

Joe P, on the corner of 81st: *Hi Tom, congratulations on your book.*

Tom nods and moves on.

In response to this "slight" I wrote the song "Not the Worlds Greatest Generation" sticking up for us baby boomers (see book's introduction).

A few years later a new coffee shop opens around the corner called Oren's, featuring 30 coffees from around the world. I go there every day. Sometimes Tom is on line in his jogging outfit. Our eyes certainly meet, but he simply does not recognize me. I realize that like myself Tom is a dragon in the Chinese zodiac and that older dragons hate younger dragons, but come on!

Then in year 36 of our failed neighborhood friendship it happens, the encounter.

My family of six is sitting at Tiramisu, a great Italian trattoria on 80th and 3rd. We dine along with 20 others, our tables lined up on the side street sidewalk. I catch Tom, coming down 80th street with his wife.

Joe P: *Tom, where are the dogs?*

He stops and with a big smile, addressing me and the whole restaurant, says …

Tom B: *We flew them out to Montana last week; the family leaves next Monday.*

We get a big wave good-by and he moves on.

Tom, truly one of the special one percent doing important work for the country.

And that's all I've got to say about that. Above: Tom & dog in Montana.

2018
VAN MORRISON

This encounter is special as Van has been a neuron alight in my brain since "forever". After all, he sails from Northern Ireland, blessing all of us with masterpieces like *Brown Eyed Girl, Moon Dance, Domino*, and so many others, including *Tupelo, Wild Nights* and *Days Like This*. His plain speaking delivery set me free as a singer. I might not be Pavarotti, but I certainly am me, telling worthy stories to who ever is listening.

But this is the last guy on earth I could imagine encountering. But it happened, and, more, it was great fun.

In February of 2018, I attend "64" at Carnegie Hall on West 57th Street in NYC. This show presents THE BEATLES in their purest form, with a bunch of Ohio guys—operating faithfully in this role for over 30 years—recreating the original BEATLE incarnation from 1964. They have a huge fan base, doing 80 world-wide shows a year. I procured four (4) fourth row center seats, bringing my wife Laura, my eldest Cody, and my almost-adopted German daughter Alexandra to the event.

I know I should get push back for asserting this, but besides Paul McCartney, no one alive knows the BEATLES better than me.

I was shattered in my one-room apartment just across Central Park, learning of John's assassination. My family attended John's Strawberry Fields death memorial in Central Park. I stood by Paul at the Saint John the Devine Cathedral on Manhattan's West Side when Linda died, not to mention my later, precious encounter with Yoko in the East Side coffee shop with my young son Joseph (covered in this book).

Plus, having written more than 200 songs myself, besides American influences like the Carter family, those BEATLE guys must have had something to do about my meager achievement. And so, as the English respectfully say: "thank you very much!"

So the "64" concert means a lot to me, and apparently to many others who flock to see this tribute band who dare to transcend being a tribute.

We get to Carnegie Hall early, though I have fourth row seats. I want to lean before the stage, a mecca of Western Civilization, where people like the violin-virtuoso HEIFITZ (above) and the culture-transforming BEATLES once performed, and I fantasize alighting the authentic guitars, amplifiers and drum kits sitting on stage that I am about to experience.

The band comes out to a full house. Each performer is masterful in his respective John, Paul, George and Ringo roles, though I have two complaints.

Being in the fourth row beneath the stage the guitar amplifiers project over our heads so that the stage mix projects somewhat like a vivid drum kit with some vocals.

More—and I cannot blame these guys for a moment—when the Paul and John guys are featured, they start their vocal deliver quite off their microphones, until they are sure their voices vibrate in the character of their ancient heroes. Only then do they move closer to the microphones, and *voila*, they suddenly sound like Paul and John incarnate, a miraculous achievement overall.

So what has all of this to do with Van Morrison?

It is rather mundane actually.

You see, at intermission, I head for the head—sort of speak—and as I progress along the stage wall, the guy behind me says "That's Van Morrison sitting there" in the first row right ahead of me.

I return from the men's room to find Van posing for a picture with the personable manager of the "64" operation, and I stay put, waiting for this photo moment to end. It does, and Van, unencumbered, leans upon the stage to breath in "Paul's" Hoffner Bass Guitars sitting on guitar stands 20 feet back on stage. Van is alone doing this, so I step next to him, also leaning on the stage, saying:

Joe: What do you think?

Van: They're great. Really!

Joe: We're lucky to witness this recreation, but I cannot hear the guitars, can you?

Van: We're beneath the speakers, so the sound projects above us.

Joe: I'm sure it sounds great further back, but I am a connoisseur and it's driving me crazy.

Van: Me too. Why don't you go talk to the sound guys?

Joe: OK, I'll try.

So I go back to the back of the hall where the sound guys sit and press my case.

Joe: Hi guys, us in the front rows can't hear the stage amplifiers which project above us.

Sound Guy: We are doing the best we can.

Joe: Well it is not just me. Van Morrison is in the first row and he asked me to say this. I'm sure the sound is perfect somewhere in the house, but could you help us out a bit down low?

Sound Guy: We'll try.

I walk back and give Van a thumbs up. The second half was great.

And that's all I've got to say about that!